£14.50 ARC
B18801811

D1582835

Dr David Chappell RIBA MA PhD currently lectures in construction, building law and contractual procedures. He has previously worked as an architect in public- and private-sector practice and has experience as contracts administrator for a building contractor. He is a regular contributor to *Building Trades Journal* and author of *Contractual Correspondence for Architects, Report Writing for Architects, Standard Letters in Architectural Practice, Standard Letters for Building Contractors,* and *Contractor's Claims.* He is also joint author with Dr Vincent Powell-Smith of *Building Contract Dictionary* and *JCT Intermediate Form of Contract: an Architect's Guide, JCT Minor Works Form of Contract: an Architect's Guide* and *Building Contracts Compared and Tabulated.*

Architectural Press Management Guides

1 The Architect's Guide to Running a Job
  Ronald Green
2 Standard Letters in Architectural Practice
  David Chappell
3 Standard Letters for Building Contractors
  David Chappell
4 The Architect in Employment
  David Chappell

Architectural Press Legal Guides

1 Professional Liability 2nd edition
  Ray Cecil
2 Building Contract Dictionary
  Vincent Powell-Smith and David Chappell
3 JCT Intermediate Form of Contract
  David Chappell and Vincent Powell-Smith
4 Small Works Contract Documentation
  Jack Bowyer
5 JCT Minor Works Form of Contract
  David Chappell and Vincent Powell-Smith

Construction Law Reports

Volumes 1–8 edited by Michael Furmston and Vincent Powell-Smith

The Architect in Employment

David Chappell

The Architectural Press: London

First published in 1987 by The Architectural
Press Ltd, 9 Queen Anne's Gate, London
SW1H 9BY

© D M Chappell 1987

**British Library Cataloguing in Publication
Data**
Chappell, David
    The architect in employment.—
    (Architectural press management guides)
    1. Architecture—Vocational guidance
    I. Title
    720'.23   NA1995
    ISBN 0–85139–798–0

Typeset by Phoenix Photosetting, Chatham
Printed in Great Britain by
Biddles Ltd, Guildford and King's Lynn

Contents

Introduction

Very few architects set up in practice immediately after achieving the requirements for registration. Although the trend towards small, one- or two-man, practices seems to be growing, most architects will spend some years as employees of a practice or of a department in an organisation. Many architects spend their whole lives as employees.

The purpose of this book is to assist in the solution of the problems of the employee architect and give practical advice for success. There are, of course, a number of excellent books of advice for the architect, but none, so far as I know, are specifically aimed at the employee. Some of the problems of the architect are common to all employees, some are specific to the architect in his capacity of skilled professional. The salaried architect must not only do the right things, he must do them in the right way. He must be professional, competent and effective and his professionalism, competence and effectiveness must be obvious.

The topics covered include obtaining employment, rights and duties, basic office skills, specific architectural skills, employment law and achieving objectives. An important chapter deals with the problems encountered when the architect begins to earn promotion and considers partnership. To complete the picture, there is a brief summary of factors to be taken into account if the architect decides to leave salaried employment and set up in practice. A list of suggested books for further reading appears at the end of the book referenced to appropriate chapters.

The text is broken down into sections to facilitate reading and to provide a handy reference. The large number of sample letters and figures should assist this process. Architects taking a post for the first time should find the contents particularly useful, but it is hoped that it will also benefit those who are already employed and are considering a move or are encountering difficulties.

Note:

o   The word 'client' is used to mean the person or firm who commissions the architect and pays to have the building constructed. To avoid confusion, the term is used even when discussing forms of contract in which the client is usually referred to as the 'employer'.

o   The word 'employer' is solely used to mean the person, partnership or firm who employs the architect.

o   For convenience, the masculine gender has been used throughout. 'He' may be taken to mean 'she', 'his' to mean 'hers', etc.

Finally, I am greatly indebted to a number of people who helped me with this book. Michael Jones Dipl Arch RIBA read and re-read early drafts and made many useful suggestions. Raymond Cecil Dip Arch RIBA FRSA kindly read the penultimate draft and saved me from several blunders. David Wylie, of DEGW, also read the penultimate draft and gave me the point of view of a seventh-year student.

Quotations from *Architect's Appointment, Code of Professional Conduct* and figures 3.11 and 7.1 are reproduced by permission of RIBA Publications Ltd., the copyright holders.

The form of Architect's Instruction is reproduced by permission of the Association of Consultant Architects Ltd., the copyright holders.

Architectural practices vary considerably. In using the advice in this book, it is assumed that the architect will modify his approach in the light of circumstances.

Basics

1.1   Terms of reference

Although the title of any book should give a fair indication of the nature of its contents, it is difficult to convey the scope without having an impossibly long title. It seems reasonable, therefore, to set out the scope of this book as a set of terms of reference. They are as follows:

○   To cover an architect's work from obtaining a post to setting up in practice. But this is not to be a detailed manual for operating your own practice.

○   To deal in some detail with the problems encountered by architects who are or will be, employed by others.

○   To cover normal architectural functions with some reference to other, less usual, forms of employment.

○   To be useful for salaried architects, surveyors and technicians.

○   To identify ways in which the architect can be successful and stay ahead of the competition. This is to be the most important theme running through the whole book. Skills which are applicable to any office worker, together with skills which are particularly relevant to architects are to be examined.

○   A reasonable assumption is made with regard to basic competence. Every architect has talents, but the talents lie in different directions with different people. The book is intended to show how you can exploit your own talents to the full so that you are successful. It is recognised that success means different things to different people. The book is laid out in a logical order. Unless otherwise stated, the reference is to some form of private practice. This does not mean that the points made cannot apply to other forms of employment, it is simply to avoid complexity in the text.

1.2   The basics of success

What follows is based on the assumption that you want to succeed. We all have different driving forces and expectations. Some people crave money or status, others simply want success for its own sake, like climbing the mountain because it is there. To many architects, success means the freedom to exercise their creative powers without interference. Even if you want none of these things, if you simply wish to have a satisfying occupation with a reasonable income, the pace of business today suggests that you cannot simply expect that to happen, or continue to happen – you must take some positive action. Everyone needs an incentive to do anything. The greater the incentive, the greater should be your chance of success. Therefore, success is often seen as the result of the principle that the hungry wolf hunts best. You can, if you wish, cultivate the drive which will push you to success.

If you are habitually satisfied with what you achieve, there is something wrong. Always be critical, to yourself, about your own work. Constantly examine what you have done and see how you could have improved. Cultivate the habit of thinking clearly, convert everything to basics, simplify and act accordingly. Muddled, over-complicated thought processes are the hallmark of the unsuccessful. The successful have learned to separate the important from the trivial and to reduce the important to essentials so that action may be taken. Be enthusiastic about your work. If you have no enthusiasm for what you do, forget it and do something else which does give you a kick.

Professional rights and duties

2.1 General duties

In your capacity as architect, you have all the duties of any other professional person. The fact that you are employed does not affect the situation except that it will generally be your employer, not you, who will bear the consequences of any breach of duty on your part. This is known as vicarious liability. Your employer will be responsible for your actions provided that you are acting in the course of your employment. Anything you do outside the course of your employment, for example, spare-time practice, is your own responsibility. Many employed architects, therefore, think that they are perfectly safe from the possibility of actions for damages in negligence. This may not be entirely correct. It is, of course, always open to an injured party to take action against any person he considers has caused the injury. Your firm's client could, unusually, take some action against you. Generally a client will proceed against the firm rather than an employee for the perfectly good reason that the firm will have more money than you and will be, as mentioned above, vicariously liable for your actions.

A particular danger, however, should be noted. If you perform a negligent action in the course of your employment which results in a successful claim against your firm, it is probable that the amount of the claim will be paid by your employer's professional indemnity insurers. It is always open to the insurers, if they think it worthwhile, to take legal action against you for the amount. This is known as 'subrogation'. It is important that you make sure that your employer's professional indemnity insurance includes a 'waiver of subrogation'. This means that the insurers undertake not to pursue their rights in this way. Although such a clause is common, you should not assume anything. Ask your employer directly.

It should be noted that a 'waiver of subrogation' on the part of the insurance company will not prevent the employer, if he is so minded, suing you for any part of a claim, such as the excess, not covered by insurance. If the insurers actually go so far as to repudiate liability, he may well be tempted to join you in any proceedings in order to minimise his own contribution. If a claim arises long after you have left the firm, when the firm itself is no longer in business and the employer dead, you may be the only person left who can be identified and sued. By that time, you may well be worth suing.

There is no easy answer. Professional indemnity insurance is not normally a realistic option for the salaried architect. You can, of course, take steps to put your assets out of harm's way although many consider that is not a proper course of action for a professional person. Certainly, if you ever set up in practice, you should ensure that your insurance covers previous employment.

With regard to the question of liability, the standard of care which you are expected to exercise is important. In order to prove negligence, a plaintiff must show that:

○   You were under a duty of care to him *and*

○   You were in breach of that duty *and*

○   The plaintiff suffered damage as a result.

The standard of care expected of an architect is different from that expected of a layman. The test is laid down in *Bolam* v *Friern Hospital Management Committee* (1957). It is basically whether you have exercised the ordinary skill of an ordinary competent man doing the same kind of work in situations involving the use of some special skill or competence. In other words, whether you have behaved in the way any other normally competent architect would behave. If you profess some additional or higher skill, that is the standard which would apply. For example, if you profess to be particularly skilled in the restoration of historic buildings, you will be expected to have skills greater than those of the average architect. In general, it might be said that you set the standard yourself. If you are architectural technician, but hold yourself out to be an architect or as skilled as an architect, it will not avail you in court to protest that you are not properly qualified. You will be judged as though you were an architect. The same is true if you hold yourself out to be able to carry out the functions of another professional, for example, a quantity surveyor. You will be expected to achieve the same standards as an ordinary qualified quantity surveyor. If you insert your name, in the space provided in the recitals to some contracts, as the quantity surveyor, it may well be held that you are holding yourself out to be a quantity surveyor or capable of exercising the same skill.

All architects, whether employed by others or self-employed, are governed by *Conduct and Discipline* prepared by the Architects Registration Council of the United Kingdom (ARCUK). The RIBA *Code of Professional Conduct* is similar, but gives more detailed guidance. This code is dicussed in section 2.4. Failure to observe the appropriate code can result in disciplinary action being taken.

2.2   Duty to the firm

A salaried architect sometimes considers that his only real duty is to carry out the instructions of his principal. If this were so, it would reduce the architect in employment to the status of a clerk. Never forget that you are a professional person with wider duties and responsibilities than the mere carrying out of instructions.

However, you do have specific duties to the firm which employs you. Some of them will be spelled out in your contract of employment (see Chapter 10), but the others will be implied.

To some extent, your duties can be summarised by stating that you must devote your energies to furthering the objectives of the practice (more about 'objectives' in section 7.1.2). That is always provided that the objectives are legal and consistent with your position as an architect. For example, you have no duty to pursue objectives if they include defrauding the Inland Revenue or supplanting other architects; quite the reverse. In such instances, you should, at the very least, remove yourself from the practice. It is to be hoped that such instances are rare.

In order to pursue objectives, of course, you must know what they are. Some firms never actually state their objectives; you are left to assume that they include such things as producing first-class service and making a profit. Other firms make a specific point of spelling out the objectives when they interview staff. If your firm says nothing, you should ask them at your interview. As a professional member of the practice, you have a duty to assist in formulating objectives if they are not clear. Unless you do this, you cannot do your best work.

Your duty also includes learning about the practice, the method of working and administrative procedures. You must know your place in the organisational structure, the person to whom you should report and the people who report to you.

Liability usually falls on the partners, even though you are negligent. Therefore, you have a duty to the partners, quite separate from your duty to others, to use skill and care in all that you do within the practice. This extends beyond any simple duty not to be negligent, because if you take longer to perform some task than strictly necessary, you are wasting money which the practice is spending on your salary.

Closely related to the question of employer's liability is the problem of your authority. In other words, what may you do or not do in any given situation? When must you refer a decision to your employer and when can you make the decision yourself? The simple, but slightly cynical, answer is that you may always make correct decisions; you may never make incorrect decisions. You should always be aware of the extent of your authority, but in practice, the precise extent of the power delegated to you is seldom defined. If you attempt to obtain a proper definition from your employer, you may be considered to be lacking initiative.

The situation will vary according to the character of your employer. If he is strong, he is likely to give you a very clear idea of the limits of your authority and be ready to support you if you occasionally exceed your remit. If you have a weak employer, he may be vague because he is unaccustomed to making clear decisions. This is most likely to be the case if you are under the supervision of an architect who is, himself, unsure of the authority delegated to him.

There is no universal rule. The best which can be done is to set out guidelines which are subject to modification depending on circumstances. It is suggested that you must always refer the following to your employer:

o   Decisions affecting the office as a whole.

o   Decisions affecting general office policy.

o   Decisions affecting other members of staff.

o   Decisions where it is clear that important questions of liability are involved.

o   Decisions relating to the unauthorised expenditure of sums of money.

Clarify the extent of your authority when you are first appointed. If circumstances change so that you perceive that your authority may be reduced or increased, seek further clarification. Be straightforward about your enquiry and you are likely to receive a clear answer. Try to understand your employer and you will learn to identify the problems about which he must be informed.

Your duty to the firm also extends to knowing your weaknesses. Never attempt to do anything for which you are not properly qualified. You will grow as a professional only by extending yourself and facing new challenges, but coping with a fresh problem is not the same as trying to do something which is clearly beyond your powers. If your employer instructs you to carry out some task for which you lack the resources or ability, you must make your position clear at the outset.

You have a duty (if you are a member of the RIBA) to comply with rule 1.0.1 of the *Code of Professional Conduct* (see section 2.4) even though, in practice, your employer will probably be most concerned.

It is essential to consider yourself as an intrinsic part of the practice, not as an individual. You must work with and through others. You have a positive duty to act as part of a team. If the office has a particular design philosophy, it should be made known to you when you apply for a post. Once you have accepted the post, you have also accepted the philosophy. You may be a genius, but you must exercise your genius within the framework laid down or seek another post. You are failing in your duty if you indulge in solo virtuoso performances of your design skill contrary to the particular preferences of that office.

An outlet for your particular genius can often be found by carrying out spare-time work, but you should only do this with the full knowledge and agreement of the firm. In turn, the firm must allow you to carry out spare-time practice so long as it does not conflict with your full-time duties. The firm's attitude to spare-time work should be made clear at your interview. Some firms encourage staff to bring commissions into the office and agree a fee-splitting arrangement.

In any firm there are some things which are confidential to differing degrees. During the time you are working in a practice, you must never reveal such information to anyone outside the practice. Indeed, such knowledge may well be restricted even within the firm: salary information, for example. You have a duty to know what is confidential and observe the confidentiality. There will be limited instances where information is so confidential that you cannot use it even after you leave.

2.3   Duty to colleagues

So far as is possible, you have a duty to act towards your professional colleagues in exactly the same way as you would act towards any other architect. In addition, of course, you have the duties of any worker towards his colleagues. The Health and Safety at Work Act 1974 says that you must take reasonable care regarding the safety of other employees. This provision would have particular relevance to survey work where some degree of hazard may be present. The Act contains detailed provisions about the employer's duty to his employees (see section 10.7 for a summary which gives some of the important provisions contained in the Act).

In addition to any statutory duty and duties imposed by the *Code of Professional Conduct*, you have duties imposed by the general law and by common sense. Your colleagues must be able to rely upon your overall competence and you must be careful not to give them negligent advice. This is an aspect of employment which is often overlooked. Architects working in the same practice often ask one another for advice. Although it seems doubtful whether you could actually be held liable if your colleague acted on your negligent advice, because he is as skilled as you are and could hardly be said to be relying on what you say, in practice, you could cost your firm a lot of money if you are careless in your comments.

2.4   Duty to clients

The primary duty of any architect is to his client. In the case of a salaried architect, he owes a duty to his firm's client by virtue of his professional status. In your relations with clients of the practice, you must, therefore, act as any other responsible professional person. You are, of course, representing the practice to an extent determined by your employer. In rare instances, you may find that your duty to your client conflicts with your duty to the practice. It should never happen and you will usually find that the conflict is perceived rather than real. If you are sure that there is a conflict, you must take immediate steps to withdraw from the situation if it cannot be resolved.

You have a general duty to demonstrate at least the competence of any other architect, a higher degree of competence if you profess it. You should, for example, be skilled in design and construction, be up to date regarding building materials and techniques, be aware of planning and Building Regulations requirements (although you have no duty to guarantee approvals) and be able to advise on contract provisions.

Specific duties will be set out in *Architect's Appointment*, if used, or in your firm's letter of appointment. The architectural practice is usually in the position of agent with limited authority. Your own responsibilities will be determined by your employer. Because the range of your responsibilities is infinitely variable, depending upon your employer, the project, the client, etc., it is assumed that your employer has given you full delegated powers. To the extent that your powers fall short of that position, the comments which follow should be similarly qualified.

If you had unlimited authority, you would be able to act for the client in any matter, not simply in regard to the project. In fact, your authority is further limited by the provisions of clauses 3.2 to 3.3 of *Architect's Appointment* which state that you:

o   Must obtain authority from the client before initiating any service or work stage. Thus you cannot simply see that another service is required – detailed negotiation with the planning department for example – and proceed, you must ask first.

o   Must not alter, add to or omit from the design without the client's consent unless in an emergency.

o   Must inform the client if the total authorised expenditure or total contract period is likely to be varied by more than a trifling amount.

The *Code of Professional Conduct* issued by the RIBA is of great importance. Its main provisions are considered below. It is, of course, binding only on members of the RIBA.

Principle One
'A member shall faithfully carry out the duties which he undertakes. He shall also have proper regard for the interests both of those who commission and of those who may be expected to use or enjoy the product of his work'.

An architect must make sure that he has the resources to carry out a commission (something has been said on this topic in section 2.2). Before entering into an agreement, he must clearly set out the terms including the extent of services to be provided, responsibilties, any limitation of liability, how fees will be calculated and how the agreement may be terminated. The agreement should be in writing and the RIBA *Architect's Appointment* should be used. He must not sub-let work without the client's permission. This is merely a restatement of the legal position that if an architect is engaged to perform a contract, he may not pass on the burden to someone else. Naturally, work can be passed from partner to senior architect or from senior architect to assistant, but if the work were to be passed to another practice to carry out, the architect responsible would be in breach, not only of the *Code*, but also of his agreement with his client. Where you are acting between parties, you must be impartial. So, for example, you must interpret the building contract fairly between client and builder. If you are called upon to decide the line of a boundary between neighbours or any other matter where both sides look to you for an expert judgment, you must give your honest opinion. This provision does not, of course, prevent you from representing the client in any such dispute against an opponent. Your duty to act fairly will arise only when both sides are relying on your judgment.

If you set up your own practice, you must ensure that any of your offices which deals with architecture is under the control, if not of yourself, of another architect. This rule prevents you from opening a branch office under the control of an unqualified assistant; unqualified in the sense of being unqualified as an architect. You may well have assistants, or even a partner, who is qualified as a surveyor or an architectural technician. The *Code* precludes them from controlling a branch office.

Principle Two
'A member shall avoid actions and situations inconsistent with his professional obligations or likely to raise doubts about his integrity.'

Any other business interests an architect might have are covered by this

Principle. If they are such as might lead the client to question his integrity because they are, or appear to be, related to the subject of his commission, the architect is obliged to disclose them before his client engages him. This applies with equal force if you are in employment and you have business interests. You must disclose them to your employer as soon as there is any question of your integrity being compromised. By far the best solution is for you to declare all your business interests to your employer when you are appointed so that he can use his judgment with regard to any commission offered to the firm. Obvious examples of such situations are cases where you already act for a builder in some other matter and your, or your employer's, client wishes to employ the builder to carry out his building work or if you own land adjacent to the client's property and over which it will be necessary to agree an easement.

If any such potential conflict of interests arises after the client has entered into an agreement with the practice, you, or your employer, must do one of three things:

o   Withdraw from the situation, *or*
o   Remove whatever is causing the conflict of interests, *or*
o   Inform the client and anyone else concerned and obtain the agreement of all parties to a continuance of the engagement.

Two examples noted in the *Code* are:

1. Where you are appointed assessor for a competition you must not subsequently take any part in the work, unless your appointment as consultant was previously arranged or if you are asked to act as arbitrator between the promoters of the competition and the selected architect in any dispute.

2. Where you are under pressure to act in contravention of the *Code*, you must report the facts to the RIBA and anyone else affected.

You must not hold yourself out to be, or practise as, an independent consulting architect if at the same time you:

o   Engage in the business of trading in land or buildings, *or*
o   Act as a property developer, *or*
o   Act as an auctioneer or house or estate agent, *or*
o   Carry on the business of a contractor or sub-contractor, *or*
o   Manufacture or supply goods to or for the building industry, *or*
o   Have a partner or co-director who engages in one of the above.

An exception may be made to this rule if you can make a full declaration to the Professional Conduct Committee of the RIBA that the combination will not prevent your compliance with the *Code* as it applies to the circumstances.

You must not hold yourself out to be independent if you or your employer is the contractor. An architect practising as both architect and contractor, cannot pretend to be independent and he must inform the client of his right to appoint another architect in such matters as quality and financial control.

You must not take any discounts, commissions or gifts (see section 4.10) as inducements to show favour to anyone. If you act as a contractor, you may take the usual trade discounts customary to the industry.

You must not try improperly to influence the granting of any kind of statutory approval. An example of this might be where you sit as a member of an advisory panel to examine planning applications and one of your own applications comes before the panel. In such a case, you would be obliged to declare your interest and, usually, remove yourself from any discussion of your own application.

Your employer must take into account your professional obligations and qualifications. He must carefully set out your responsibilities and liabilities. Among other things, he must;

o   Allow you appropriate authority and responsibility.

o   Give you suitable public credit for your work.

o   Allow you to engage in spare-time practice provided that, in turn, you inform him.

o   Allow appropriate opportunities for you to continue your professional development.

o   Co-operate in the educational requirements of such students as he may employ.

If you are in practice, you must not have a partner or co-ordinator who is disqualified from registration or expelled from the register or disqualified by reason of explusion from any other professional body, without the permission of the RIBA.

Principle Three
'A member shall rely only on ability and achievement as the basis for his advancement.'

This portion of the *Code* is designed to regulate the ways in which an architect can obtain work. The *Code* encourages you to play your full part in bodies such as amenity societies, concerned with the quality of the environment. You may criticise what you believe to be harmful, shoddy or inappropriate, provided that no malice is involved and the criticism does not contravene any rule under Principle Three.

You may not give discounts or gifts for the introduction of clients or work. If you operate as a contractor, you may give all the customary trade discounts.

An architect may quote a fee for carrying out a commission. Before he does so, however, he must have enough information to know what the project entails and what services the client requires. He must not offer a quotation unless his client so requests. In effect, therefore, he is allowed to compete on the basis of price. He is not allowed to reduce his fee to take account of a quotation which the client has obtained from another architect. This is to reduce the possibility of a 'Dutch auction' taking place. Many architects do not care to participate in competitive quotation although it is now common. It is very much a matter for the individual architect and his approach to the business of obtaining work. Fee quotation involves many hours of consultations with the client and fee calculation which may prove a complete waste of time.

Provided that the quotation is not on a competitive basis, there is nothing to prevent an architect entering into negotiations with the client after he has quoted. It may be that he can reduce his fee to take account of particular factors of which he was unaware or he may suggest a reduction in the services he is offering. The basic position is that he must not attempt to supplant another architect. Thus, you may not approach a prospective client and offer your services if you know that he has already entered into discussions with another architect. If your client proposes a fee basis which you feel unable to accept because to do so would call into question your integrity or your professional obligations, you are obliged to withdraw from the negotiations and report the facts to the RIBA. The situation might arise in any number of ways. It could be, for example, that your client is attempting to link your remuneration to some other financial activity rather than pay an agreed fee for the work. If you are in the position of working for an employer and he is relying upon you to negotiate an agreement for him with another independent consulting architect, you are obliged to respect the obligations of the independent architect under the *Code*.

If an architect is approached to undertake a commission which he knows is being handled, or has been handled, by another architect, he is obliged to notify the original architect of the fact (Fig 2.1). His obligation is, in fact, to make reasonable enquiries to ascertain whether such a situation exists. This can be a delicate task (Fig 2.2). The object of the procedure is to enable the original architect to take whatever steps may be appropriate. In the majority of cases, the original architect will do nothing other than acknowledged the notice. If the client has omitted to pay the fees of the original architect, there is no obligation to refuse the commission, but it may well be considered prudent to seek further information from the client and possibly ask for some payment on account before beginning work (Fig 2.3)

There is an exception to this rule if the client can show that it would be prejudicial to prospective litigation to give notice to the original architect. It is for the client to advance some very convincing arguments to this end. If an architect is engaged as an expert to advise on some matter, he cannot, thereafter, be used as an arbitrator in any related dispute.

An architect may let prospective clients know of his availability and the extent of his experience by any means provided that the information given be factual, relevant and neither misleading nor unfair to others nor discreditable to the profession. Thus, an architect may send a letter stating that he knows a prospective client intends to build and offering his services (Fig 2.4) or he may put advertisements in newspapers or magazines. The *Code* does not prevent him from appearing on television to talk about his buildings. He may send material to the media on his own work or on general architectural topics and he may pay to have his work published or exhibited.

An architect may put his name outside his office or on buildings under construction provided it is done unostentatiously. He is encouraged to sign the finished building in a permanent way, with his client's agreement of course. You may also allow your employer, even if he is not an architect, to use your name and professional affix on his letterheads and literature as consultant or staff architect.

An architect may employ an external public relations consultant to handle that part of his business, but he must send a declaration, signed by the consultant, to the RIBA to ensure that he will do nothing to contravene the *Code*.

The final part of the *Code* prevents an architect from entering an architectural competition which has been declared by the RIBA to be unacceptable.

The *Code* is more than simply a set of rules for fair dealing. It points out the high standard of behaviour which is expected of a professional person in a position of trust.

2.5   Duties to third parties

When architects talk about their duty to third parties, they tend to speak in terms of the public at large. An architect's duty is perceived as consisting very largely of a duty to preserve and enhance the environment. There can be little doubt that you have such a duty. When you design something, you must have regard to its impact on the general environment. If you fail to exercise adequate thought in this direction, however, the worst which can happen is usually delay in obtaining planning permission. If you already have obtained planning permission, the finished building may receive some unfriendly comments from amenity societies and the like. If it is really bad, you may find it featured in the professional press. It is unlikely that your employer will be sued simply because your building design fails to 'fit in' because such a failing tends to fall into the category of the debatable.

Fig 2.1
Letters from architect to another architect regarding former engagement.

Dear Sir

[*Heading*]

I have been approached/instructed [*omit as appropriate*] by [*insert name of client*] to undertake the above project.

I understand that you were engaged on this project at one time and you should take this letter as notice in accordance with Principle 3, Rule 3.5 of the RIBA Code of Professional Conduct.

If you have any comments, I should be pleased to receive them.

Yours faithfully

Fig 2.2

Letter from architect to client regarding other architects.

Dear Sir

[*Heading*]

In order to comply with the RIBA Code of
Professional Conduct, I am required to make
reasonable enquiries to discover if you have
previously engaged any other architect on this
project. I consider that this letter fulfils that
duty.

If another architect has been involved at any time,
perhaps you will let me have his name and address so
that I may inform him that I am now acting for you.

Yours faithfully

Fig 2.3

Letter from architect to client if previously engaged architect notifies some difficulty.

Dear Sir

[Heading]

I have been informed by [insert name of previous architect] that [insert the nature of the problem, e.g., 'he has received no payment from you for his previous involvement in this project'].

Although this is not a matter which concerns me directly, you may wish to appraise me of the full circumstances of the situation. If you wish to make no further comment, that is your prerogative.

[You may wish to add]

In the circumstances, however, and without passing any comment on the liabilities of the previous engagement, I think that it is reasonable to request a payment on account of [insert amount] before I begin/proceed with [omit as appropriate] the work.

Yours faithfully

Fig 2.4
Letter from architect to prospective client, offering services.

Dear Sir

[*Heading*]

I was interested to hear that your company intends
to [*insert nature of development*]. Obviously, I
have no idea whether you have commissioned an
architect for the work. If not, this letter is to
let you know that I should be delighted to discuss
the project with a view to handling it for you.

A copy of 'Practice Information', my illustrated
brochure, is enclosed for your information. From it
you will see that this practice is experienced in
carrying out work of the kind you appear to have in
mind.

If you consider that a meeting would be mutually
beneficial, please let me know.

Yours faithfully

You have other duties, however, to third parties which may cause more difficulty for you, or the firm which employs you. The duty of care which you are expected to exercise extends to all those who you can reasonable foresee might suffer injury due to your actions, for example, persons who might use your buildings. On occasion, it can extend further, and you or your employer can be liable if the person suffering injury only does so because of some abnormal reaction on his part. These duties are covered by the law of tort which lays a general duty on you to be a good neighbour. In this context, your 'neighbour' may be some future purchaser of your building or simply the man in the street. It is clear that your duty is oner- ous. This is not the place to attempt to outline the law of tort. Sufficient to say that your duty is to have a good working knowledge of the law. Ignor- ance is no excuse.

You have no duty to the contractor under the building contract, because your employer is not a party to it. You do, however, have the ordinary duty of care towards the contractor as to anyone, else. Moreover, this duty could lead to problems because you are in such close proximity to the con- tractor and his men. You must not give negligent advice when visiting site, for example. You must be particularly wary of any situation which may endanger health and safety. In general, of course, the contractor will first look to your employer's client if there is any contractual problem. If you are at fault, you are in breach of your duty to the client. You may be sued in negligence by the contractor, however, if you fail to perform your duties properly under the contract, but this would be an action in tort. You have no duty to the contractor to find defects in the work because the building contract lays no such duty on the architect and, therefore, an action in tort on such grounds would be ill-founded, however, you prob- ably have a duty to warn the contractor if it is clear that he is making a major mistake which will cause him expense. You do have a limited duty to the client to find defects in the work, but such duty arises out of your employer's contract of engagement with the client.

You also have duties imposed by statute. For example, duties in con- nection with the planning authorities and statutory undertakings as laid down in the appropriate regulations. An example of this is your duty to comply with the Building Regulations.

2.6   Summary

o   The fact of being employed does not remove any of your profes- sional duties.

o   Your employer will be vicariously liable for your actions provided that you are acting in the course of your employment.

o   While employed, you may not be safe from actions for damages.

o   Check your employer's professional indemnity insurance provision.

o   You must exercise a higher standard of care than that of a layman.

o   You are governed by the ARCUK *Conduct and Discipline*. If you are a member of the RIBA, you must also observe the *Code of Professional Conduct*.

o   Your duty to the firm involves more than carrying out instructions.

o   You have duties to your colleagues under the Health and Safety at Work Act 1974.

o   Your primary duty is to the client.

o   Your employer's position is one of agent with limited authority.

o   Your duty to third parties arises mainly in tort.

o   You also have statutory duties to third parties.

Obtaining employment

3.1 The broad field of employment

3.1.1 Introduction

Whether you are a newly qualified architect looking for your first appointment or an experienced architect looking for a change, you may find that obtaining employment is not easy. It is relatively easy to get a job, but getting just the job you want is more diffcult. Twenty years ago, things were different, but that is another story.

To some extent, the principles of obtaining employment are similar whether you are an architect, a solicitor or an ex-company director. The field is known as Professional and Executive. But, as an architect, your aspirations and job requirements are unique and demand a rather different approach to job hunting. This chapter attempts to set out the principles applicable to your own job search so that you start in the correct way and end by getting the post you want. For the most part, the principles are widely known and widely neglected. In the last analysis, of course, the successful outcome depends upon you, your particular talents, experience and personality, but neglect of the basic principles will put you at a severe disadvantage. We have all experienced the interview at which the 'whizz-kid' gets the job we wanted. Often, he fails to fulfil expectations and quickly whizzes off to another, better, job somewhere else. The common denominator is that this type of person knows how to set about finding a post, applying for it and making a good impression at an interview. You may not feel very impressive, but the art of finding the right post is very much the art of presenting yourself in the best possible way.

3.1.2 Areas of employment

Architects tend to see the job market as divided roughly between private practice and local authority work. It is to these areas that most effort is devoted. Although there is no doubt that these two categories embrace the majority of architectural posts, there are others which should not be ignored. Table 3.1 lists a selection of fruitful job sources and the list cannot be considered to be exhaustive. It might be useful to consider a few of the areas listed:

Private practice
This type of office appeals to many architects for a variety or reasons:
o   The type of work.
o   The variety of work.
o   The range of duties.
o   The feeling of involvement.
o   The chance to take responsibility.
o   The opportunities for advancement to partnership status.
Private offices, of course, vary in size just like any other office. There are a few very large multi-disciplinary offices, a large number of medium-sized practices and an increasing number of very small offices consisting of two or three architects or architectural staff. They vary also in the type of work they do and their reputations. Some are very prestigious indeed and much sought after and, at the other end of the scale, there are offices which are

| **Table 3.1** |
| Sources of architectural appointments |
| o   Private practice |
| o   Local government |
| o   Central government |
| o   Area health authorities |
| o   Statutory undertakings |
| o   Nationalised industries |
| o   New town and other development boards |
| o   Housing associations |
| o   Universities |
| o   Ecclesiastical authorities |
| o   Banks |
| o   Broadcasting and TV companies |
| o   Large companies |
| o   Building contractors |
| o   Manufacturers of building components |

content to produce a majority of small works which seldom if ever get featured in the technical and professional press. The scope is, therefore, very wide, but getting a good job in a first class practice is a very competitive business.

Local authority
Many local authority architect's departments have a very high reputation. Unfortunately, the number of such offices and of posts within them has been tending to shrink over the last few years. None the less, there are still such offices in all parts of the country, sometimes merged with local authority building departments, but operating as clearly defined departments in their own rights. The scope of work in such departments is clearly not so great as in private practice. They do, however, offer a considerable amount of job satisfaction. The opportunities for advancement tend to be along well-defined lines and there is little chance that you could obtain the sort of rapid movement which is possible in many private offices. On the other hand they still offer a fair degree of security, if that is your main concern.

Nationalised industries
These tend to offer rather more specialised experience, depending upon the industry. Some of them have regional architect's departments which are rather similar in general organisation to local authority offices. The disadvantage lies to some extent in their specialisation. After several years working for a nationalised industry, you may have a little more difficulty moving elsewhere than if your experience is broader in nature, unless, of course, you move to an office where that particular expertise is required.

Universities
Many universities employ their own architects to deal with minor building works and maintenance and to liase with consultants. The departments are not very large, but often the numbers and variety in types of buildings are considerable. Whether the involvement is primarily with new or old buildings depends upon the university and the policies pursued by government from time to time.

Ecclesiastical authorities
The majority of the architectural work carried out in relationship to churches and chapels is entrusted to private firms. Church inspections and maintenance, however, are often the responsibility of the diocesan surveyor and there are limited openings for architects of a practical turn of mind.

Large companies
Some large companies have their own architect's departments. The type of work depends on the type of company. It might consist mainly of renovation and alteration work to company buildings, but there is the possibility of handling new work such as offices, workshops, laboratories, etc., and housing accommodation for company employees. Many companies have branches in other countries and overseas travel is another attraction.

Building contractors
Most large contractors and many medium-sized contractors employ their own architects. The work varies considerably. If the firm is a design and build operation, very large projects may be handled. Firms engaged in mainly speculative work often find it more convenient to maintain a small architectural department, not only to carry out design work but also to give general assistance on contract work from time to time. An architect employed in this capacity can have a varied and satisfying career. The possibilities of advancement to director level are well worth consideration. One disadvantage often associated with working for a contractor is the split in duty between the building firm and the ultimate purchaser of the building. Some architects would not consider such a post because they would find it impossible to reconcile what they see as a conflict of interest.

Manufacturers of building components
Product design and development is a field which few architects consider seriously, but the enormous range of manufacturers should not be discounted as a source of employment. Such firms sometimes advertise for architects; others probably need architects, but do not realise it.

3.1.3 Variety of employment

Although the bulk of this book is intended to help architects carrying out what can perhaps be termed the traditional architectural function, you should not forget that there are many job opportunities for the talented individual in related spheres of activity. Table 3.2 lists some of them. It is encouraging to see that most schools of architecture now actively promote a first degree in architecture as a basic qualification for a number of related occupations. If the practice of architecture does not give you the satisfaction you once knew, it may be because your true vocation lies elsewhere. You should give the matter careful consideration. Every architect develops particular interests and expertise and it may be that your particular interest should be pursued to the exclusion of the traditional architect's role. Interests in interior design and model making are good examples. Although Table 3.2 is very brief, it may be useful to consider some of the options:

Planning
Many architects are drawn to planning because it is really an extension of their skills. Many planning departments of local authorities employ architects as well as architect planners, particularly in the fields of development control and historic buildings. Ideally, you should obtain a planning qualification, otherwise you have virtually no chance of useful promotion. Posts are not easy to get at the present time. There are planners in private practice, of course, sometimes in conjunction with an architectural practice, but again, a planning qualification is needed. If planning is your real interest, taking time out to secure the necessary qualifications is your obvious next step.

Surveying
Like 'engineering', 'surveying' is rather a vague term. Quantity surveying is one obvious branch, though seldom attractive to architects. Perhaps this is because it is seen as more like mathematics and economics than building. This is, of course, a false view; rather like saying that architecture is simply drawing pictures. Although, in theory, architects should be able to perform many of the quantity surveying functions, you are unlikely to be taken seriously unless you take the trouble to become properly qualified. Building and land surveyors are quite closely related to architects, and building surveyors in particular often deal with most aspects of the construction process. An architect may often be an acceptable candidate for a building surveyor's post. Land surveying is rather more specialised

Table 3.2
Related disciplines

- o Planning
- o Surveying
- o Project management
- o Contracting
- o Estate management
- o Estate agency
- o Valuation
- o Interior design
- o Furniture design
- o Graphic design
- o Perspective drawing
- o Model making
- o Sales representative for architectural products
- o Architectural writing and journalism
- o Lecturing

and, although not beyond the capabilities of the architect who has a special interest, additional qualification is desirable. Municipal building surveyors are employed in building control offices. For architects with an interest, the required qualifications should be relatively easy to achieve while doing the job.

Project management
Something which architects do all the time. There are different types of project management and a number of firms who now do nothing else. It is thought by some to be the single most significant development in recent years. If you enjoy contract administration and have good organisational ability, this may be where your vocation truly lies.

Contracting
More and more architects seem to be attracted to contracting. It requires a very practical mind and, like project management, good organisational ability. It is possible, but unlikely, that you have the skills required to be a good site agent, but there are many other posts within a contractor's organisation for which an architect of the right temperament is ideally suited.

Estate management
Normally more concerned with overall building maintenance than new building. Particular skills are required to create and operate planned maintenance procedures. These skills, however, can be acquired if you have sufficient interest.

Estate agency
The principal skills required are valuation and sales. Surveying, structural and general constructional skills are valuable assets which the architect is well qualified to bring to this field. Additional qualification is desirable.

Valuation
Closely allied to estate agency. It is a special skill which can be only partly taught. Many architectural pratices carry out valuation work and, if the work interests you, there is no reason why you should not carry your knowledge into other fields. Again, an additional qualification improves your credibility.

Interior design
Although, strictly, this is just one aspect of architectural design, it has tended to develop into a separate discipline. A good sense of colour, graphics and form is essential.

Perspective drawing/model making
Many architectural offices produce their own models and perspectives. There are, however, firms which specialise in this field and produce presentations of all kinds. The firms are fairly limited in number, but if you have a talent and interest there will be openings from time to time.

Sales representative for architectural products
An architect with the right personality can make a successful career in this field. If the firm is big enough, the opportunities for advancement can be very good. A variation is technical representative, but the sales element can never be far away. It is not an occupation for sensitive souls, for reasons with which all architects will be familiar.

Architectural writing and journalism
The opportunities are limited, but if you enjoy expressing yourself in writing and you can do it well, you should not overlook this avenue.

Lecturing
There are plenty of opportunities, but starting salaries can be depressingly low. The moral, therefore, is to start as young as is consistent with having something useful to say. Many lecturing posts carry research or consultancy responsibilities and should suit you if you have a large amount of self confidence.

3.2   Finding employment

3.2.1 Self-assessment

When you apply for a post you are actually trying to sell yourself. Just as a salesman cannot market a product effectively unless he knows all about it, you cannot market yourself unless you know your strengths and weaknesses.

Architects should be adept at the art of selling. After all they are regularly called upon to make presentations of their schemes to clients. The first step is to sit down and carry out a self-appraisal (Table 3.3) so that you thoroughly know the 'goods'. Do it in note form following the headings below:

o   Formal qualifications. This should be easy. Include your degree or diploma or both, your professional institute membership, membership of any other professional institute and any other degrees. Avoid listing membership of minor institutes which may give you the right to certain letters after your name, but which tend to dilute your main qualification.

They give the impression that you are scratching around for something to put down.

o   Experience. Do not be vague. If you are recently qualified, your experience will be slim, but make the most of it. It is useful to put down experience as follows:

Your most recent appointments (say during the last five years).

Your duties in each post. This is not nearly as important as:

Your achievements. Think very carefully about this one, it is an important selling point. Have you played a major part in the design of a really good building? Have you ever brought a contract back from the brink of disaster? Have you introduced a system which made your office more cost-effective? In order words, have you done anything which makes you outstanding in a particular field. You may become quite depressed about this section of your self-appraisal. It is not unusual to feel that you have achieved very little. What you are probably feeling is that you have not achieved as much as you would have liked – not the same thing at all. Take it slowly, go through all the work you have done and you will probably be surprised at the extent of your achievements.

Table 3.3
Self-appraisal

o   Formal qualifications
o   Experience
     Most recent appointments
     Duties in each post
     Achievements
o   Talents
o   Personality
o   Career objectives
     Job satisfaction
     Pay
     Advancement
     Responsibility
     Ancillary: Location
                Security
                Working hours
                Opportunity for initiative
                Office environment
                Personality of partners
                Type of work
                Design philosophy

o   Talents – the things you do best. What do you most like doing?
What do you least like doing?

o   Personality – how do you get on with your colleagues, your
superiors, those under your charge? How do you relate to contractors,
representatives and officials in public bodies? What do you consider to be
your most vulnerable points? It might be your age or your youth and inex-
perience or difficulty in mastering CAD. It is important to acknowledge
them at this stage so that you can be prepared if the subject arises during
interview.

o   Career objectives. The next step is to decide what you really want
from your career. Presumably, you decided to become an architect in the
first place because you wanted to participate in the creation and maintenance of a delightful, satisfying and durable environment for the benefit of
everyone who will inhabit or pass through it. Ultimately, that should be
what you are striving to achieve. All your actions should be carried out
with that end in mind. Efficient management and competent design work
are not ends in themselves. Few people actually sit down and plan their
careers, but it pays to do so even if things do not work out according to
your plan. It is not unknown for architects to drift into satisfying, well-
paid appointments, but do not count on it. The following are a few
headings to guide your thoughts:

—   Job satisfaction. Most architects want this, but it means different
things to different architects. What kind of architectural work do you want?
Very small or very large projects, mainly designing, contract administration, technology, new work or rehab? Try to define your 'ideal' post.

—   Pay. Decide how much you need to move. Would you be prepared
to accept the same salary, or less, than you are getting at the moment to
obtain the job you want? How much money do you actually need and
what difference would it make if the job were two hundred miles away?
Job satisfaction and pay are the two vital ingredients of a good job.

—   Advancement. Think hard whether this is very important to you.
Most people have a desire to progress, but not all. What are you prepared
to do or relinquish to secure promotion? Although the absence of good
prospects may suggest that a job is not worth having, it is generally true
that a good architect will make his own prospects.

—   Responsibility. If you want to be totally responsible for everything
you do, you are aiming to be top of the tree. Does status matter to you or
are you more interested in practising your own particular skills?

—   Ancillary. There are many other things which you might have on
your list of ideal job attributes. They may be very important to you, but ask
yourself whether they are as important as job satisfaction and pay. Try to
keep your requirements simple and getting the job you want will be easier.
Among the other things which might influence you are the following:

Location.
Security.
Working hours.
Opportunity for initiative.
Office environment.
Personality of partners.
Completing this checklist should clarify your thoughts and, incidentally, reveal certain facets of your character which you may not have acknowleged before. The complete self-appraisal is the unrefined raw material which you have to use to find employment.

3.2.2 Opportunities

You have considered the areas of employment and the variety of employment open to you. You have a very clear idea of your own capabilities and the kind of post you are looking for. The next stage is to consider how to set about locating the sort of job vacancies that you want. It is always possible, of course, that someone will telephone you unexpectedly and offer you just the job you require. Although this happens more frequently than you might think, the principal ways of locating vacancies are:

o   Advertisements in the professional, technical or local press.
o   Speculative approaches to potential employers.
o   Word of mouth, through contacts in other offices.

Remember that it is possible to persuade an employer that he needs just your kind of architectural expertise. A number of architects have found their niche in this way. There are techniques to help ensure that you, and not someone else, are successful when applying for a post.

3.2.3 Answering advertisements

This is probably the way in which most architects find employment. Besides looking at the obvious professional press, do not neglect the less obvious construction journals which also have advertisements for architects occasionally and which may advertise posts that are not aimed specifically at architects (see section 3.1.3). National and regional newspapers are a fruitful source of jobs. Some small practices rarely advertise beyond regional level. Some large organisations have their own magazine or journal in which they advertise vacancies before they appear nationally. Local authorities, in particular, sometimes have a policy about advertising 'in house' as a first step. It is, of course, impossible to keep abreast of all such advertisements, but if you have a clear idea of the post you want, it pays to scan as many relevant publications as possible. Remember that advertisements on a national scale are likely to attract more applications.

The kind of advertisement you will encounter varies widely. Posts described as 'assistant architect' or 'qualified architect' suggest that the originators have not read the RIBA Practice Note on the subject of job titles. Some advertisements give masses of information, others hardly anything at all beyond the job title. A salary may or may not be quoted. Large organisations commonly ask you to write for further details and an application form while private practices usually ask for a CV. The techniques for preparing these are dealt with in sections 3.2.6 and 3.2.7. The first rule of answering advertisements is to do exactly as they request. It is pointless sending a CV if they want you to fill in an application form. It simply creates a bad impression. It suggests that you are incapable of understanding what you read. Some firms still ask applicants to fill in forms or write to them in handwriting. It may strike you as a trifle weird in this age of electronic typewriters and computers, but follow instructions. Generally, employers are just trying to find out if your writing is decipherable, but it is possible, in the case of a large company, that they have retained a graphologist to comment on your personality. There are some employers who think they can read your character in your handwriting; a clear neat hand indicates a logical neat person, etc. Without passing any judgment on such theories, it is suggested that you simply write in your usual hand, taking care that it is legible. Unless you are required to submit your application in handwriting, it is better to have it typed. Some letters cannot be standardised. The examples included in this chapter fall into that category. They are included simply to show you the sort of letter which could be sent; they lack an indication of *your* individuality. The letters must be shaped by you in relation to the particular circumstances.

o   If a CV is required, send one with a covering letter (Fig 3.4).

o   If there is an application form, write for it (Fig 3.5) then send the completed form back with a covering letter (Fig 3.6).

If selection is to be by means of completed application forms, it normally makes little difference whether you apply immediately or wait until just before the closing date because all the applications will be considered after the last date.

Private practices asking for a CV seldom state a closing date. It often pays to submit your application promptly.

Some firms invite you to telephone for an informal chat or to write or telephone for further details. If you know that you have a good telephone manner and if you are confident and quick thinking, by all means telephone. You may virtually secure the post on that basis, making the interview a formality. When telephoning a prospective employer, be sure to have some notes prepared as if for an interview, with questions ready. If you are at all nervous about telephoning, write instead. The telephone can magnify vocal mannerisms and the listener concentrates on the voice

Fig 3.4
Letter from applicant to employer, enclosing a CV

Dear Sir

[*Job title and reference number, if any*]

In response to your advertisement for the above post, I enclose my CV as requested.

I am attracted to this post because [*insert reasons - see section 3.2.7*].

My experience/skills in [*insert particular field*] appears to relate directly to your requirements and I should welcome the opportunity of meeting you to demonstrate my suitability for the post.

Yours faithfully

because there is nothing else to distract him. There may be a bad line, the person on the other end of the telephone may seem abrupt and a thousand and one things can conspire to upset what you fondly imagined would be a friendly chat. What you are seeking is a face to face meeting where you can relate to the interviewer. So if you have any doubts, leave the telephone alone.

3.2.4 The speculative approach

You may think that writing to a firm of architects to offer your services is a waste of time. Whether it is or not will depend upon the firm and its circumstances at the time you write. Such an approach can be successful. There are four possible scenarios:

o   Your approach will be rejected out of hand.

o   The firm may be about to advertise a vacancy and they may decide to interview you before they incur the expense of inserting the advertisement in the press.

o   You may impress the firm sufficiently for them to create a post especially to use your particular expertise.

o   You may impress the firm sufficiently to secure an interview which may lead to a post in the future when they have the right opening. Firms do not enjoy the hassle of full-scale interview sessions. They do not like to waste the time or the money. If they have a post and they know of someone who can fill it, they will often contact him. If you have persuaded them to interview you a few weeks before and you have impressed them, they will contact you.

Your reason for making a speculative approach may well be that you know the firm by reputation, you admire their work and, therefore, you want to join them, but they are not advertising any vacancies. There is nothing demeaning about a speculative approach. The recipient should be flattered. Some firms never have any need to advertise because architects are anxious to join them.

Avoid sending anything that looks like a mass-produced application in these circumstances. If you make a number of such approaches, make sure that each application is given an individual bias. At the very least address the letter to the person in the firm who deals with staffing. You can easily find out who this is by telephoning the firm and asking the receptionist for his name and qualifications. Address your letter 'Dear Mr . . .' and finish it 'Yours sincerely'. It should be brief and to the point (Fig 3.7 and 3.8). There are no hard and fast rules regarding whether you should include a CV or not. Generally, it is probably better not to send the CV. Your letter should give just enough information to convince the recipient that it is worth while meeting you. Remember, the purpose of appli-

Fig 3.5
Letter from applicant to employer, asking for an application form

Dear Sir

[*Job title and reference number, if any*]

I read your advertisement for the above post with great interest. My experience/skills in [*insert particular area*] appear to be directly relevant to your requirements.

I should be pleased to receive an application form and further details of the post.

Yours faithfully

Fig 3.6
Letter from applicant to employer when returning application
form

Dear Sir

[*Job title and reference number, if any*]

I enclose my application form for the above post.

I was particularly interested in [*stress some aspect
of the post related to your own experience*].

I am attracted to this post because [*insert reasons
- see section 3.2.7*].

Yours faithfully

Fig 3.7

Letter from applicant to employer if speculative approach 1

Dear Mr [*insert name*]

I have admired your work for some time and I am keen to join your organisation.

Although you are not advertising for additional staff at the present time, I believe that my experience/skills would prove a valuable addition to your office.

[*Insert a brief outline of your achievements*]

I should welcome the opportunity to visit you and discuss the ways in which I can contribute to your work.

Yours sincerely

Fig 3.8

Letter from applicant to employer if speculative approach 2

Dear Mr [*insert name*]

I am interested in joining an organisation which
will make full use of my talents.

[*Insert a brief outline of your achievements*]

If you consider that it might be mutually
advantageous to take the matter further, I should
welcome the opportunity of meeting you to enlarge
upon my achievements and relate them to your
requirements.

Yours sincerely

cations is to secure an interview. The purpose of the interview is to secure the post.

Speculative approaches by telephone should not be attempted unless you are very confident of your ability to sell yourself (see section 3.2.3). In communications, a telephone conversation is halfway between a letter and a face to face meeting. In a letter you can say just as much as you wish. You cannot be drawn into a hurried response. At a meeting, you can moderate or emphasise what you say by gesture and facial expression and read similar signals from the interviewer. In comparison, the telephone can be a very coarse instrument of communication. Its danger lies in the fact that it seems to give a better picture of both parties whereas in fact it gives only a partial picture, and that perhaps the worst part.

3.2.5 Contacts

Everyone has contacts. You will have some in the architectural world, many elsewhere. If you let it be known that you are seeking another appointment, the results can be surprising. You may get an approach from a firm who had not thought of approaching you before because you appeared to be settled in your present firm for life. More often, a contact can sometimes tell you of vacancies which have not yet been advertised enabling you to make a successful speculative approach yourself. The old adage that 'it's not what you know, but who you know that matters' has more than a grain of truth.

There are a number of other avenues for seeking the kind of job you want, for example, University Appointments Board (if you are a graduate), RIBA at national or regional level and placement consultants. The latter can be very effective, but you have to keep up pressure on them. Typically, you will be asked to fill in a registration form which they try to match with prospective employers. Some specialise in architectural appointments. They collect their fee from employers not from you. Whether a placement consultant appeals to you will depend upon how clear you are about the sort of post you want. If you are looking for any kind of architectural work, they can be very useful. If you have strong views about the development of your career, it is probably better to make your own approaches.

3.2.6 Career history and CV

CV stands for curriculum vitae – the story of your life. What most firms actually mean when they ask for a CV is a career history. They do not want to know about your early childhood or anything which is not abso-lutely relevant to your application.

Ideally, the CV should occupy no more than one sheet of A4 paper. Even though you are submitting a career history, head it 'curriculum vitae' if that is what the prospective employer asks for. An example is shown in Fig. 3.9. Try to write the CV to suit the post for which you are applying. Keep the layout clear, typed if possible and remember the following, which may make all the difference between success and failure:

o   If you think your age might be a problem, leave out your date of birth. Employers sometimes have a preconceived notion about a fifty-year-old as opposed to a thirty-year-old applicant. At fifty, a man is less likely to move again, he is experienced, skilful and can be just as enthu-siastic as a younger man. The only disadvantage with an older man is that he may be slightly slower than his younger colleague.

o   Include degrees and professional qualifications, but not 'O' and 'A' level results. They are merely steps on the road to your professional qua-lifications. The only exception is if your 'O' or 'A' levels indicate an apti-tude for something which is not strictly architectural but which could prove useful to a potential employer. An example is if you are proficient in languages and the firm is engaged in work abroad.

o   Put down your present appointment first, then work backwards. Ten years ago is ancient history. Simply list appointments before that time.

o   Emphasise achievements rather than duties and be brief.

o   If the titles of any of your previous posts are obscure, amend them to be comprehensible to the reader.

o   If you were self-employed for any period, the firm will wonder why you are not still self-employed. Are you a business failure? Include a con-vincing reason for giving it up.

o   Otherwise do not put reasons for leaving a post. Particularly, do not ever say that you were made redundant. Although, these days, there is no reason why it should, mention of redundancy gives prospective employers the feeling that you may not be worth employing.

o   Do not include your present salary. You are worth what you are worth to the firm to which you are applying, not £500 more than your last salary; you might have been grossly underpaid.

o   Under 'additional information' include only items which are stric-tly relevant. The fact that you are a keen fisherman is not relevant. It sug-gests a loner. Involvement in a local society indicates that you are public spirited and you have contacts which might prove useful to the firm.

The above is only a guide. There may be good reasons to ignore some of the advice. It is up to you to use your judgment. Applying for a new post should be approached with the same skill and care you would bring to any other im-portant task. There can be few things more important than your career, but it is surprising how many applicants dash off an application in a few minutes. The recipient will probably give it the same sort of cursory treatment.

Fig 3.9

Curriculum vitae (or career history)


```
PERSONAL DETAILS

 Name:            Inigo Jones

 Address:         1 Dedetmy Way, Sleaping, Kent, SL1 4AL

 Telephone:       (0101) 101010

 Date of birth: 15 March 1946.  Married

 EDUCATION AND QUALIFICATIONS

 1963-69          University of Chester, Department of Architecture
                  1966 Bachelor of Architecture
                  1969 Diploma in Architecture
 Professional:    1971 RIBA, ARCUK

 EXPERIENCE AND ACHIEVEMENTS

 1983-            SENIOR ARCHITECT with Skechit Quickly Associates,
                  of Pons.  Responsible to partner for group of
                  5 architects and technicians engaged on the
                  design and production drawings for research
                  laboratories, contract sum £4,500,000.  My duties
                  include collation of the brief, research,
                  instigating a programme of work, supervision of
                  staff and administering the contract, which is
                  presently on site.  A very tight design programme
                  was stipulated, of 4 months from Inception to
                  starting work on site.  I successfully achieved
                  the programmed dates and liaised with consultants
                  to keep within the estimated cost.  The work on
                  site is half way through an eighteen month
                  contract period and the contractor is two weeks
                  ahead of his programme.
                  In this post I have also supervised the design
                  of an abattoir (£500,000) and a small theatre
                  (£300,000).

 1978-83          SENIOR ARCHITECT with H. Cluch-Pensel Partnership,
                  of Hythe.  Responsible to partner for group of
                  3 technicians working on a variety of buildings
                  including a housing estate (£200,000), group
                  surgery (£150,000), and redevelopment scheme for
                  part of town centre (£600,000).  I successfully
                  introduced a system of standardised schedules and
                  details which saved 10% of production drawing
                  time.  My experience in laboratory work was
                  instrumental in the partnership securing
                  commissions for a continuing series of medical
                  and scientific buildings.
 1973-78          ARCHITECT with Pseudo-Scientific Co. Ltd,
                  of Canterbury.
 1969-73          ARCHITECT with Middling District Council,
                  of Middling.

 OTHER INFORMATION

                  Chairman of the Sleaping Civic Society.
                  Member of a local cricket team.
                  Keen interest in photography.
```

3.2.7 The application form

Many application forms are exceedingly badly arranged. Remember to use the form for your own advantage. Read any information you have about the post carefully before completing. Answer all questions in the spirit of the information you have been given, using the same words if possible. For example, if the information calls for an architect with a 'flair for design', include the phrase in the application form. Complete the form neatly but fill the available space adequately. Attach additional sheets to detail your experience if the space is too small (it usually is). Most application forms are straightforward, but some forms have one or more questions which may prove difficult to answer. A selection of such questions and outlines of possible answers are given below. The details, of course, will depend upon the individual.

What do you consider are your greatest strengths and weaknesses?
This offers both a chance and a trap. Do not be modest, state your strengths, whether they are the much sought after 'flair for design' or project management or the restoration of old buildings. If there is space, give an example. This is an opportunity for you to emphasise your achievements. For example, 'I directed the design team on XYZ Building'. This can be very effective if XYZ is a well-known project. The second part of the question is a trap. It is an invitation for you to give the firm a reason for excluding you from interview. On no account must you put down such things as 'I tend to get bored with office work' or 'I find it difficult to arrive on time in the morning'. These things may well be true, but they will not help you secure an interview. It is possible to turn such a question to your own advantage by stating as faults what some others might easily see as good points. For example: 'I tend to concentrate on detail, but I am capable of seeing the broad picture' or 'I become frustrated if every member of the team is not pulling his weight. I deal with it by face to face discussion with the person involved'. It is not suggested that you invent your weaknesses; merely that you take something about which you are maybe a shade too fanatical, state it as a weakness (which it is) then say how you overcome it.

What has been your greatest disappointment?
Do not say that you have not got as far as you would have liked in your career, you failed to solve the cladding problem on XYZ Buildings or nobody likes your new hotel design. Use the same technique as for 'weaknesses' above. The perfectionist is always bitterly disappointed that his near perfect conception is not actually perfect. So your greatest disappointment might be that your award-winning design had some minor

planning problem or the technology was not available to do what you wanted or your innovative office costing scheme will not be ready for implementation until after you have left.

Why are you applying for this post?
Another opportunity for you to relate your achievements and show how they apply to the post for which you are applying. Stress the aspects of the firm or organisation which you find most appealing, for example: reputation for good design, efficiency, new technology, etc. These points will impress the prospective employer. He will be unimpressed if you say that you are applying because the office is near your home or you need the extra money.

What are the major ways in which you consider that you can contribute to the work of this organisation?
As above.

Reasons for leaving your present post?
Do not say that you have been fired, made redundant or had major policy disagreements with your boss. The reasons for leaving should be because you are anxious to further your career and you consider that the best way to do that is to join the firm to which you are applying.

Which of your duties gave you the most satisfaction?
Another opportunity to state your achievements. Beware of appearing to be too much of a specialist, unless that is what the advertiser requires.

If you are offered the post, where do you see yourself in ten years' time?
This is always a difficult one. The totally honest answer might be that you have no idea. The safest way is to stick to generalities. Stress your progress so far and concentrate on your personal development as a contracts administrator, designer, technologist, etc., which you see continuing in logical progression depending upon the opportunities which are offered to you.

Describe, in detail, how your experience relates to this post
This question often appears in very much longer form. It is not an invitation to write your life story. Be clear and to the point. Put down those achievements which are most closely related to the work you will be expected to do. Many architects ramble in answer to this question. 'In detail' simply means that the employer wants actual examples to be quoted.
A few further points to remember about application forms:

appointment only is to be made, there will usually be between four and seven interviewees. It is common to take candidates in alphabetical order. If your name begins with ABC or WXYZ, therefore, you will probably be seen first or last which are supposed to be the best positions. Sometimes other considerations affect the order, such as distance of travel. The middle of the list is supposed to be the worst place because a candidate in this position becomes confused with other candidates in the mind of the interviewer. You will have to impress that bit more if you are to secure the post. Most architectural posts call for you to take along visual materials of some kind to the interview. There are exceptions to this of course, for example, if the post for which you are applying is purely administrative. Some architects, too, refuse to take any drawings, etc., to an interview as a matter of principle; presumably on the view that, being architects, they have no need to show their quality, it is taken for granted. That is a very mistaken view. Whether or not you are requested, always take visual material with you to show, not just that you are competent but also, that you think along the same lines as the firm you hope to join. You may take some or all of the following:

o   Drawings. They should be flat not rolled and prints not negatives. Choose drawings to suit the post. For example, if the firm does a lot of housing, take drawings of a domestic character; if the post is for an architect to design warehouses and factories, take your industrial work. Unless the post is very specialised, take some other work also to show the breadth of your expertise. If you are just or recently qualified, you will have to take one or two projects you did while training, but be ready to face keener criticism of such work and be ready with your answers. Unless the post particularly indicates otherwise, take only one or two working drawings, but make sure they are good. There is nothing wrong with taking drawings which have been produced by someone else provided that you make the fact clear. It may be that you had an important supervisory and co-ordinating role. Be prepared for keen questioning in that case.

o   Photographs. They must be first-class large prints, but you will have to work hard to prove that you had a key role to play in the building if they are unsupported by your drawings.

o   Glossy brochure about you and your work. In theory this is very good, but it does give the impression that you make a habit of attending interviews.

o   Complete file of correspondence concerning the post. You must take this. Include a copy of your career history or application form and a list of the points you want to make. Some architects think it bad form to take notes to an interview. They are mistaken. The interviewer will certainly use notes, there is no reason why you cannot use notes also.

The above is merely a guide. There is no point in taking a portfolio of drawings if your last role was purely administrative and you are applying for a similar post. One last thing you can do in preparation for your interview is to remember to take a 150mm scale rule and soft pencil.

3.3.2 The interview

You should arrive about a quarter of an hour early. If you arrive later, you will have no time to compose yourself and examine the reception area where, no doubt, the firm's work will be displayed. If you are very early, you may become nervous. If it is one of those interviews where you have to wait with a group of other candidates, listen more than you talk. You may be able to assess the strength of the competition.

Local authorities and large organisations will have a special form for claiming expenses. Smaller firms are unlikely to have such a form, but they may be willing to pay your expenses. In that case, list the expenses with your name and address and leave them with the secretary. It is not something to bring up during the interview.

There are two basic types of interview:

o   One to one.

o   Committee or panel.

The one to one interview offers you the best chance to establish a relationship with the interviewer and, therefore, the best chance of obtaining the post. A committee interview can be very difficult. There is usually a chairman, and each member asks questions in turn. When answering questions reply directly to the person asking the question. Try to remember the names of the members when they are introduced and use them during the interview. You can never be sure of the relationships between members of a committee. They may be more interested in impressing one another than in you. Your interviewer will almost certainly be another architect, but it is not invariably so. If there is a panel, some members may be personnel, managerial or, in the case of a local authority, councillors.

The *RIBA Handbook* sets out some useful guidelines for interviewing from the point of view of the employer. It forms a useful guide for you also because you know the kind of things the employer is looking for. Not all interviewers use this system of course, but they must base their assessment on similar grounds. The interview appraisal form from the handbook is shown in Fig 3.11.

Interviews may be structured or unstructured. The first follows a pattern set by the interviewer, the second rambles and gives you the opportunity to set the pattern. The latter form of interview is very common because interviewing is a skill which few employers bother to learn properly. A typical interview often runs as follows:

o   The interviewer chats for a few minutes to help you relax.

o   He gives you a description of the firm.

Fig 3.11
Interview appraisal form

Applicant's name :

for appointment as :

**Interview
Appraisal Form**

Grading : **A**—Indifferent, **B**—Adequate, **C**—Good, **D**—Outstanding

	A	B	C	D	Notes
Impression :					
appearance					
manner					
speech					
health & general fitness					
Qualifications, Experience :					
general education					
professional training					
experience: (a) research					
(b) design					
(c) job management					
(d) cost control					
(e) administration					
Brains & Ability :					
general intelligence					
judgement & foresight					
skills: (a) words					
(b) figures					
(c) draughtmanship					
(d) organising ability					
Motivation :					
initiative					
enthusiasm & stimulus					
interests: (a) practical					
(b) intellectual					
(c) social					
Adjustment :					
stability, control, reliability					
acceptability to others					
influence on others					
attitude to architecture					

○   He gives you a description of the post advertised.

○   He questions you on your application form.

○   He puts half a dozen technical questions.

○   He looks at your portfolio with more questions.

○   He gives you time to ask questions.

Arrangements vary greatly. The interview may take place across a desk or around a conference table or sitting in easy chairs with coffee. Quite a lot depends upon the type of job for which you are applying. For your first post you may well be interviewed formally across a desk. As you progress to more senior posts, the interviews tend to become less formal as the interviewer wants to get to know you better. This is particularly true in the case of posts which may lead to partnerships. Points to bear in mind:

○   Speak slowly and clearly.

○   Look at the interviewer, do not look down.

○   Be enthusiastic.

○   Think before you answer.

○   Do not make a present of your expertise. If you are asked to solve a problem, try to show that you know how to set about solving it without actually doing so.

○   If you are not asked to open your portfolio, open it anyway when you are asked for your points.

○   If possible, begin your answers by saying 'yes' or 'no'. Always elaborate on your answers, but not too much.

○   Never miss an opportunity to display your experience, achievments and skill.

○   Ask some questions which show that you have looked at the firm's work, but do not be too critical unless you have already decided that you do not want the post.

Remember that the interview is a two-way affair. It may not seem that way in practice, but it is. You have to decide whether you want the post. If you are good at what you do, the employer will be anxious to impress you. Be positive in your approach. Stress your achievements and your interest in the post for which you are applying.

Every interview contains some awkward questions. In some cases, the interviewer himself would not know how to answer. The ability to deal with awkward questions depends upon your experience and your confidence. Always humour the interviewer. Never tell him that a question is silly. If you are really at a loss for an answer, compliment him on devising such a difficult question and admit that he has you beaten. This device is particularly effective in a panel interview. Although awkward questions can never be entirely forseen (one reason why they are awkward), the following is a selection of such questions which regularly make their appearances at interviews:

Why do you want to leave your present post?
Furtherance of your career and joining the firm to which you are applying are acceptable answers, being fired, made redundant or seeking more money are not.

Do you think that you are too young/too old/too inexperienced for this post?
Stress your interest in the post, restate your achievements and skills.

Given the opportunity, how would you reorganise this firm to make it more efficient?
This is a really silly question. The only reason for asking it is to see if you are silly enough to attempt an answer. Say that you would be delighted to answer the question if they will give you sufficient time to study the firm. If appropriate, explain how you reorganised some aspect of your present firm.

Who is your favourite architect?
Be ready for this one. Say who and say why. Do not use jargon. The why is more important than the who. It does not matter that the architect is not a favourite of the architect who is interviewing you. Effective things to admire are attention to detail and planning.

Why did you stay so long with your last firm?
Emphasise the additional responsibility you have taken over the years and your progression within the firm. Do not say that you were on the point of leaving many times, but stayed because you were offered more money. Among other things, the employer may think that your present application is just a ploy to increase your salary again at your old firm. This question inevitably leads to the one about reasons for leaving at this stage. Your reasons can only be that this seems to be the right moment in your career pattern. Be warned, however, that employers will want to know why such a long-serving member as yourself does not rate a partnership at your old firm. Only you know why, but do not criticise your present firm.

It seems to us that a person with your particular skills/experience/qualifications should be (doing something else)
This is tricky. It may also be true. Presumably you want the post for which you have applied. Why do you want it? That is the answer you must give. Emphasise your interest in the post.

Why do you think you are the person for this post?
Another opportunity to stress your achievements in your last post and relate them to what you know of the requirements of this post.

How would you motivate others?
Books have been written about this. Read one of them. Put very simply,

motivating someone else involves getting him to want to do what you want him to do by letting him see it is in his own best interests.

What salary are you looking for?
Try not to answer this question. It is really up to the employer to make you an offer, but in any case, salary discussions should not take place until the end of the interview. What you are prepared to accept as salary will depend upon a number of factors:

o   Your own personal circumstances.
o   Frequency of salary review.
o   Possibility and frequency of bonuses.
o   Company car.
o   Telephone expenses.

As a general guide, it does not usually pay to accept less than you want for the promise of something indefinite such as promotion in two or three years' time. Bonuses too, have the habit of disappearing unless you have the percentage written in as a definite part of your remuneration. If you have no alternative but to state the salary you require, either:

o   State a range (e.g., £10,000 to £12,000).
o   If you are confident that you can command a particular salary, ask for it, but not tentatively.

The list of awkward questions is endless. In addition, you may be asked to sit what amounts to a short examination, spot mistakes in a drawing, undergo a psychological test. You should co-operate fully with the employer's whims unless you have already decided that you do not want the post. Remember, what appears to you to be a silly waste of time may be something in which the employer places the utmost faith. Try to put yourself inside the interviewer's mind. It is more than likely that he is an architect like yourself, but he may have been educated in a different way and his experience of the practicalities of architectural practice may not be yours. So put emphasis on what you have in common and play down the rest.

As in any other meeting, misunderstandings can arise during the course of an interview which can be the reason why you are not offered the post. To overcome the possibility, you should ask a question at the end of the interview to expose any reservations on the part of the employer. It can be phrased in many different ways, but it should be something like: 'Did any points arise during the course of the interview which lead you to believe that I am not suitable for the post?' If the answer is 'No', the post should be yours. If the answer is 'Yes', you have the opportunity to correct the misunderstandings. The employer cannot really refuse to give you an answer.

3.3.3 After the interview

If all candidates are being interviewed on the same day, it is common practice to announce the result shortly after the last interview is completed. In other cases, you will be informed by post. You should hear the result in about a week. If not, consider writing a letter to find out the position (Fig 3.12). You may not have heard because:

o The post has been offered to someone else and the employer is waiting for his acceptance before notifying you.

o The employer is unsure whether any of the applicants is suitable.

o Points raised during the interview have caused the employer to rethink some basic office policy.

In each case, you will increase your chances of obtaining the post if you send a carefully worded letter emphasising your interest in the post and in the firm. Even if the post has been offered to someone else, he may turn it down and your letter pushes your name to the front of the alternatives. Do not telephone. You may embarrass or annoy the employer and force him into making a quick decision which is unlikely to be favourable.

3.3.4 Letter of appointment

The letter of appointment and your acceptance form the basis of your contract of employment.

3.4 Starting work

3.4.1 Introduction

There are a number of matters which you may not have had an opportunity to mention during the interview, but which are important to you. They are:

o Overtime.

o Private work.

o Expenses.

o Insurance.

o Pensions.

It is difficult to draw a precise line between what should and what should not be discussed during an interview. With the exception of expenses, all the above matters are included in the checklist in Table 3.10. It is anticipated, however, that even if you mentioned them, the dicussion in depth will not take place until you take up your post. Once in the new office, you must settle any outstanding points without delay. If you wait more than a few days, you will be at a disadvantage.

Fig 3.12

Letter from applicant to employer after interview

Dear Mr [*insert name*]

[*Job title and reference number, if any*]

Following the meeting I had with you on the [*insert
date*] when we discussed the above post, have you
made any firm decision about this vacancy?

I am still very interested in joining your office
and you will recall [*insert what you see as the most
significant point to emerge from the interview*]
which I see as the key contribution which I can make
to your work.

Yours sincerely

3.4.2 Overtime

You will be expected to work overtime at certain periods when there is a heavy workload or when there is a temporary 'crisis' which demands attention. Just how overtime is handled will depend on the particular office. Although it is better to be slightly understaffed, regular overtime is not a good idea. Everyone needs time to relax and recharge batteries otherwise tiredness becomes the order of the day and mistakes occur (see section 7.3.2).

If you find that 'temporary' crises are occuring on a more or less per-manent basis, there is something wrong with the office. It is a symptom of an underlying fault. If you are in a position to diagnose the problem and suggest a way of dealing with it, you may make a name for yourself.

Some offices attempt to repay overtime work by allowing time off in lieu. This is seldom really satisfactory unless overtime working is a rare occurence. Generally, people who work overtime have difficulty in finding a space in their workload to enable them to take time off. The choice of time off or payment can be useful. Although payment for overtime working should be on a higher scale than usual – perhaps one and a half to twice the normal rate of pay – some offices will try to pay the standard rate for overtime. You should resist such an approach from the start.

Exactly how you deal with overtime will depend on the office, the regula-rity of overtime, the reason for the overtime and your own career aspir-ations. It by no means follows that the employee who is always willing to work overtime speeds his own promotion. Although it hardly needs saying that all the members of an office should co-operate and work as a team, you must not allow yourself to be taken for granted.

3.4.3 Private work

Something has already been said about private work in section 2.2. In general, you must be allowed to carry out private work unless there is a specific term in your contract of employment forbidding it. You must inform your employer and ensure that any part-time work you do is kept quite separate from your office duties unless you reach an agreement to the contrary with your employer.

Problems sometimes arise with regard to your clients. You must make clear to them that you are acting in a personal capacity and not on behalf of your firm. Moreover, you should not accept any private commission from a client of your employer. It is not always easy to ensure that your activities do not affect your employer. The safest system is to clear all pro-posed private work with your employer *before* you accept it. Even then, it is difficult to know if some of your client's activities affect the practice for which you work. If you should find yourself in a position which suggests conflicting loyalties, remember that you are bound by the professional code and act accordingly. If you always act in a straightforward manner, you will rarely encounter insuperable difficulties in your relationships. Some practices encourage salaried staff to bring all work into the office and they recognise such introduction by means of a fee-splitting arrangement. If you see your future as part of the firm for which you currently work, you will probably bring all work into the office in any case. If you are accomplished at obtaining commissions, it is unlikely that you will go unrewarded. If, on the other hand, you see your future in setting up your own practice, you will probably wish to retain all your own commissions to help build up a reputation and a body of work against the day when you decide to set up on your own.

A great advantage of bringing all work into the office or carrying it out yourself under the office banner is that you will have the protection of the office professional indemnity insurance. Private work is carried out at your own risk. If you are negligent, your client will look to you for damages. In theory, therefore, you should carry the proper amount of cover for all your private work. The reality is that you will be unlikely to be able to afford such cover. It is a point which many salaried architects engaged in private work seem to ignore. All may be well during the time when you are employed and your client knows that you are not worth suing, but the situation can be different if you do set up in practice or become a partner and your earlier negligence results in a heavy claim for damages. The answer is to get good advice from your insurance broker before you commence any private work.

3.4.4 Expenses

The general law will imply a term in your contract of employment that the employer will indemnify you against any expense which you reasonably incur in carrying out your duties (see section 10.2.1). Within that general statement, however, there is considerable scope for difference in practice. Such things as car allowance or mileage allowance will certainly be mentioned at interview, but the precise figures will only become apparent when you start work. Some firms are very generous and others very mean. If your firm is mean, you should carry out your duties strictly in accordance with the rules laid down. Do not fall into the trap of subsidising the firm by using your own car if you are not fully reimbursed. Travelling is probably the most important expense, but there are others which may affect you from time to time. Subsistence (meals and hotel expenses) and entertainment policy must be settled before you incur any expense. It is impossible to give precise guidance because firms differ so much. In general, you can assume that a good firm will have a sensible approach to the question of expenses. A firm which has an unreasonable attitude to expenses probably has an unreasonable attitude to other aspects of your employment and, since you are unlikely to be able to change such an attitude, you should seek your fortune elsewhere.

3.4.5 Insurance

You must check on the professional indemnity insurance arrangements. Make sure that there is a waiver of subrogation on the part of the insurance company. It is usual, but make sure. Another essential insurance is cover against accidents. It is the simplest thing to trip and break a leg or suffer some other incapacitating injury while on firm's business. Your firm should have such insurance, but make sure and in what terms. If you are away from work due to injury, you need to know that, at the very least, your salary is protected. Surprisingly few people take the trouble to enquire. A useful insurance which many firms provide either free or at a reduced premium is private medical insurance. It enables you to plan non-urgent operations or treatment to fit in with other commitments and ensures that you are restored to full working fitness in the shortest possible time. If you are expected to make some contribution, you should carefully read all the conditions and weigh the considerations before deciding to join. Remember that the Inland Revenue consider such insurance, if provided wholly or partially at the firm's expense to be a 'benefit', on the value of which you will be liable to pay tax.

3.4.6 Pensions

If you work for local or central government, you must retire at a predetermined age. If you are employed by a private company, you may be allowed to continue working so long as you are capable of making a worthwhile contribution. A fixed retirement age is a very artificial thing. There are some people who welcome the opportunity to retire in their fifties, some whose physical or mental condition forces early retirement and others who seem to reach their peak performance late in life and dread the thought of retirement. Many of the 'giants' of the architectural profession continue working for the whole of their lives simply because work is pleasure and without the opportunity to practise architecture life loses much of its attraction.

Most salaried architects, however, must face the fact that they will retire sometime during their sixties. Although it is perfectly possible to carry on a small private practice during retirement, it is not something easily started at that point. When you are in your twenties or thirties, you may think that one day you will have your own practice, but even if you do, you must still make provision for retirement.

It makes sense to consider your pension from the moment you start working. There are a great many pension schemes available. Before you do anything you must consult your insurance broker and spend some time considering the implications of the various options. The field is highly specialised and the following comments merely outline the position.

The state pension scheme is available for every salaried employee. It is in two sections:

o   A basic pension.

o   An additional pension.

There are some disadvantages and you are advised to read the appropriate pamphlets issued by the Department of Health and Social Security (see Appendix A).

An employer may elect to contract out of the additional part of the state pension scheme and all employees must be given the opportunity to discuss any alternative proposal before it is implemented.

An employer may decide to introduce an additional pension scheme for the benefit of employees over and above the state pension scheme. In some instances, the employer may pay all contributions to achieve maximum tax advantage.

At present, a person's retirement income cannot exceed two-thirds of his or her final salary (as averaged over the last few years of service).

Any salaried architect considering taking part in a company pension scheme should bear in mind the following:

o   Is it possible to transfer the pension with a change of firm without disadvantage?

o   Is there any cash sum for death in service?

o   Is there any cash sum for retirement?

o   What difference will a cash sum on retirement make to retirement income?

o   The tax position.

o   Are contributions steady, increasing or fluctuating?

o   Provision for widow.

o   Would some other personal pension plan be more advantageous?

There are a great many personal pension schemes available for the self-employed and to persons who are employed, but not members of a company pension scheme. Again, the advice of an insurance broker should be sought.

3.5 Summary

o   There are many opportunities for architects.

o   There are many opportunities for people who have an architectural training, other than the purely architectural .

o   The first thing to do is find out about yourself.

o   Then plan your career.

o   Trawl widely in your search for a suitable post.

o   Take care in answering advertisements.

o   The object is to secure an interview.

o   The speculative approach can reap rewards.

o   Your CV or Career History should be one-page long.

o   Fill an application form with detail and take care over difficult questions.

o   Prepare for the interview by finding out as much as you can about your prospective employer.

o   Prepare a list of questions.

o   Take material with you.

o   At the interview, be enthusiastic about yourself and the post.

o   Be confident and co-operative.

o   Be ready for awkward questions.

o   Leave salary until the end when it may be a formality or irrelevant.

o   If you have not heard the result within a week of the interview, write and emphasise your interest in the post.

o   The letter of appointment and your acceptance forms a contract.

o   Treat overtime working with caution.

o   Private work can be too much of a liability unless you intend to set up in practice one day.

o   The question of expenses demands a sensible approach from both employer and employee.

o   Check your firm's insurances.

o   It is never too early to start considering your pension requirements.

Basic office skills

4.1   Introduction

Many of the basic skills you will need to work in an architect's office are
similar to the skills you would need in any office. There are some obvious,
and some rather subtle, differences. Schools of Architecture seem reluctant to include training in such skills as part of their curricula.
There is no doubt that an architect who is adept at working the office
systems has a head start over his colleagues. The office skills to be dealt
with in this chapter are not merely the correct ways of doing various jobs;
rather the most effective ways of doing them. It is usually assumed that
architects will acquire skills as part of their office-based training. The
truth is, of course, that some do and some do not. A very few architects
seem born with just the right approach to dealing with in-office problems.
The rest of us acquire the skills over a long period during which we constantly revise our views and take on board the advice of our elders.
It is important to know what not to do; when, in fact, to do nothing, how to
appear effective at all times. If you wish to make your mark in an office, you
ignore such skills at your peril. Remember, if you wish to advance your career,
it is not enough to be effective, everyone must know that you are effective.

4.2   The telephone

4.2.1 Location

In some offices, every architect has a telephone by his board. In others,
there may be just one telephone between a group of architects. In all but

the smallest offices, incoming calls are filtered through the telephonist. For maximum efficiency, you should have your own telephone. If you have to share a telephone, it is best located in some neutral place, such as on an empty desk, so that the user does not disturb others. If the telephone is on your desk, most of the calls you receive and which interrupt your work will be for others. They will then delay you further while they answer the call. Given the choice, always opt to sit as far away as possible from the telephone so that someone else has to answer it.

If most calls are for you and the telephone is on a colleague's desk, he may become understandably frustrated. He may even offer to change places with you. Reject such offers unless changing places gives you distinct advantages such as better drawing facilities, access to technical files, etc. Suggest, instead, that the telephone be moved to a neutral position. The neutral position must have adequate flat reference space to enable drawings to be consulted. In most offices, such a flat space becomes cluttered up with discarded drawings, old journals, literature and models. Keep it clear ruthlessly. Your colleagues should see the wisdom of your actions. If they do not, it is because they are lazy and inefficient. You will not, and you should not try to, be popular with such people. Your success depends upon your being popular with clients and, therefore, your boss, not your lazy and inefficient colleagues. That is not to say, of course, that you should actively try to be disruptive. Be diplomatic, but when that approach fails, know how to stand firm.

4.2.2 The telephonist

The telephonist is a key person in any practice. Give your telephonist every consideration. She (telephonists are usually, but not always, female) is the first contact between a prospective client and the firm. She has to be bright, cheerful and helpful. If you are bright and cheerful in your dealings with your telephonist, you will find that you will get maximum co-operation in return. Do not treat her like a piece of office equipment. 'Please would you get me . . .' achieves far better results than 'Get me . . .' Be unfailingly courteous and mindful of her difficulties. A partner will always get his calls put through efficiently simply because he is a partner. You can achieve the same result by showing that you know how to treat the telephonist as a human being. If you doubt the truth of this, observe how the telephone is a source of frustration to the bad-tempered, curt or arrogant architect.

Very small practices, of which there are a growing number, seldom have a full-time telephonist. Sometimes the lady who does the typing doubles as telephonist, more often it is left for one of the architectural staff to answer the telephone. In such a situation, it is imperative that the telephone is not on your desk or you will spend more time answering it and taking messages than producing architecture.

If the practice is composed of less than three people, it may well be equipped with an answering machine to cope with those instances when everyone is out of the office. Although an answering machine is preferable to leaving the telephone completely unmanned, it is only just preferable. Ideally, the message left on the tape should state when someone will be in the office to return calls. That means making a new message tape on every occasion that the office is to be left empty. Try not to become the answering machine yourself.

Callers who leave a request for you to call back will probably have very little faith that you will call back promptly. Do just that. If you do not get into the habit of returning all taped messages as soon as you return to the office, all your clients will do what many of them do already – hang up as soon as they hear the machine.

4.2.3 The internal telephone

Few offices actually need an internal telephone facility. It may be useful if the staff are dispersed in several offices on different floors of a building. In most small offices, however, it is just an unnecessary affectation. If you have an internal telephone, use it sparingly. A face-to-face chat with your colleague in the next room will usually achieve better results. Some people think that an internal telephone is useful because it saves time; not only the time it takes to actually walk and see a colleague, but also the time wasted when the simple query turns into a ten-minute chat. The error in this line of reasoning lies in the fact that, not only is it quite possible to chat for ten minutes on an internal telephone line but, without it, you will probably save your queries until you have enough to make it worth while to get up and walk to another office. The internal telephone can develop into a kind of toy to be used to while away a boring afternoon without regard to the fact that the recipients of calls may not wish to be interrupted.

4.2.4 Answering the telephone

It is amazing how many people do not know how to answer the telephone. If you simply say 'Hello!', the caller has to enquire who is speaking or ask again for the person already asked for at the switchboard. It all wastes time.

If you are answering for the office, i.e., not through the switchboard but direct on an outside line, say 'XYZ and Partners, good morning.'

If you are answering for a department of a larger organisation say, 'Architects' Department.'

If you are answering on your own telephone or one which you share with two or three others, just give your name. At one time it used to be accepted that you simply gave your surname, e.g., 'Smith speaking.' Nowadays, it is more usual to strike a more informal note with, 'John Smith speaking.' A very annoying and time-wasting caller is the secretary who has instructions to get you on the line for her boss. Once she has actually got you on the other end of the line, you may be kept waiting for several minutes until she manages to put her boss through, because he may have wandered off to another office. A more annoying variation is when the secretary asks for someone who is not in the office. On being told this, she will ask you to hold the line while she enquires whether anyone else can take the call. This procedure can be repeated several times, and all the while you are being kept waiting. There is only one real ploy you can use to effectively overcome this annoyance. When you are told to hold the line, count five and, if the line is still silent, hang up. It may annoy whoever is calling you, but they will usually ring back, this time with the person who wishes to speak to you on the other end of the telephone. People who use this system of telephoning are showing you extreme discourtesy by implying that you are not as busy as they are. You may, of course, wish to show more tolerance to clients. That is a matter for your own judgment. Be aware, however, that many people play the 'telephone game' as a means of establishing, before they begin to speak to you, that they are 'one up'. If you have established sufficient rapport with your own telephonist, you can ask her to make sure that she disposes of the secretary before she puts the call through.

An important part of answering the telephone is taking notes. These take two forms:

o   Notes of your own calls to be put on the appropriate job file for future reference.

o   Messages for other members of the firm.

Notes of your own calls may be valuable in the future if a dispute should arise. If the office does not have one, you should have some simple forms produced to make the recording of your own incoming and outgoing calls easy (Fig 4.1). Always make a note of messages for colleagues. Again, they should be written on forms specially prepared for the purpose (Fig 4.2). If you simply scribble a message on any spare piece of paper, the chance of its reaching the file are remote. Have the telephone slips printed on paper of a distinctive colour.

4.2.5 Making a call

Make all your calls directly to the person to whom you wisk to speak. If you have to go through your own telephonist, be ready, waiting to pick up

Fig 4.1

Form for recording telephone calls

```
Telephone call to/from ...........................

Subject .........................................

Date ...................



Further action ...........


Signed ................... Date ...................
```

Fig 4.2

Form for recording telephone messages

```
Message for .....................................

From ........................

Taken by ....................

At ................. am/pm  on ................Date



Action taken .............

Signed ................... Date ...................
```

the telephone the moment she rings you. Otherwise, you will annoy the person you wish to speak to in exactly the way outlined in the previous section. Always ask to speak to the person you know will be able to help you or get things done. Do not ask to speak to his secretary or his assistant. It wastes time and suggests that you are unsure of your own position.

Be brief and to the point. Do not ramble. If necessary, make notes of the points you wish to discuss. If you need a file, have it near you when you telephone. Do say who you are before you say anything else. Do not waste time on pleasantries about the weather, golf, etc., unless you have established a friendship with the person you are calling and you know that he considers such pleasantries an indispensible preamble to a telephone conversation. A client may well warrant a more informal approach.

Remember, particularly when telephoning someone you have never met, that the telephone is a very imperfect means of communication. It does not convey facial expression, or mood. It can exaggerate accents. The person you telephone may have several people in the room with him or be in the middle of drafting an important letter. It is easy for a telephone conversation to turn into an argument. Never pick up the telephone in annoyance. Stay calm and reasonable.

4.2.6 Timing

You can find that you are wasting more time, and therefore firm's money, on telephone calls than anything else. The need to make an urgent telephone call should be a rarity. Calls made after 1.00 pm are cheaper than those made before. Try to develop a system of making and taking telephone calls. With the assistance of the telephonist, you can condense the whole of your calls into two periods during the day. Ask her not to put calls through to you, but to take a note of the caller and the telephone number and to let you have a list of all callers at two set times, say 12.00 and 4.30 pm. You can then return all calls one after the other and make your own calls at the same time. Leave as many as possible until 4.30 pm anyway because you will be checking correspondence at about this time. You will have large uninterrupted periods of time during the day for getting on with your work. The exceptions to the above will be those callers who state that their business is urgent or any names you have left with the telephonist because you are waiting for their calls.

If you operate a system such as the one described, you will get a reputation inside the firm and out, for being efficient and busy. A great deal depends upon the telephonist, who should be dedicated, enthusiastic and well paid.

4.3   Correspondence

4.3.1 Introduction

Many architects find that writing letters is the single most difficult thing they have to do. It is very tempting to pick up the telephone instead of writing a letter. There are many instances, however, when there is no sensible alternative to written communications. These instances are:
o   Confirming oral conversations.
o   Answering questions.
o   Giving information.
o   Requesting information.
o   Giving instructions.
The style of writing will vary depending upon the individual writing and the person for whom the letter is intended. Thus letters to contractors, local authorities, manufacturers and suppliers should be quite formal, but letters to clients can be suited to the client's own particular character. This is all a matter for your own taste and judgment, but there are basic principles which will help you to write effectively.

4.3.2 Effective writing

If you are to be effective, you must learn to think clearly. Before you write any letter you must ask yourself:
o   Is the letter really necessary?
o   What do I want to say exactly?
A common fault is to sit down to write a letter hoping that inspiration will assist you. It is generally better, if you have time, to think about what you are going to say while you are doing other things so that, when you begin to write, you have some thoughts to put down.
Always make notes unless your letter is very short indeed. Your thoughts may well be very muddled, particularly if it is to be a long letter. No matter, write them down anyway. Then spend some time putting the notes into order. Try to make the letter flow naturally from one subject to another. It is a good idea to confine generalities to the beginning of a letter and follow with specifics. If the items you wish to cover are totally unrelated, number them. It makes answering your letter much easier. If you have some bad news to impart, or a disagreeable question to ask, put it in the body of the letter between items of a more positive nature. If you have a really important question to ask, give it a paragraph to itself at the very end or at the beginning of the letter, where it will not be overlooked (see Fig 4.3).
Use short sentences. It helps understanding. If the letter is important

Fig 4.3

Schematic layout for letters

```
References

Name and address                     Date

of recipient


Dear Sir [or name]

Heading

Refer to: telephone conversation  ⎤
          meeting                  ⎥
          discussion               ⎬ Location
          visit, etc.              ⎥
      or: thanks for letter received ⎦


General points                     ⎬ Introduction


Itemised points in logical order   ⎤
or order of previous letter        ⎥
                                   ⎬ Body
or numbered, including bad news    ⎥
or contentious points              ⎦


Important question                 ⎤
                                   ⎬ Closer
or vital point                     ⎦


Yours faithfully [sincerely]


for and on behalf of

[name of person or firm]
```

Fig 4.4

If you change your mind

Dear Sir

[*Heading*]

I refer to my visit to site yesterday and confirm my oral clarifications as follows:

[*Insert clarification, then add:*]

I particularly wish to draw your attention to [*insert the matter about which you have changed your mind*].

With the benefit of mature reflection, I believe that my original opinion was not the best view that can be taken of the matter. With this in mind, please ignore my comments on this subject yesterday. Instead [*insert what you want the contractor to do*]

Yours faithfully

draft and re-draft several times until you are satisfied that the meaning is absolutely clear. Try to read your own letter as if you were on the receiving end. Try to be positive. Do not use vague words. Always appear totally reasonable, remember that your letter, however innocent, may be used as evidence in court one day. The biggest charge levelled by contractors against architects is arrogance. It may be difficult to avoid appearing arrogant when refusing the contractor's request or taking him to task for some breach.

Never write in anger or, at least, do not let your anger show in the letter. On the other hand, do not write apologetically if you have nothing for which to apologise. Too often one sees the phrase 'I regret to inform you . . ' when the writer has no regrets at all. It is better to write a letter which is cold and formal than to write one in which the meaning is obscured in a welter of surplus verbs and adjectives.

Avoid any temptation to be devious. Be as honest and straightforward in your letter-writing as you would be about any other branch of your profession. A reputation for total integrity is a valuable, but fragile, thing. If you are confirming an oral clarification, do it clearly and thoroughly. Do not attempt to leave out something which you said at the time, but afterwards regretted. It is not worth it. In such a case, state quite simply that you have changed your mind (Fig 4.4)

4.3.3 Answering letters

In answering letters, stick rigidly to the point unless there is some overwhelming reason for departing from this principle. Most of the letters you receive will probably be short, containing only one or two items requiring a reply. There are some instances when you may not want to reply:

o   If you have already answered the point in previous correspondence and your correspondent is simply trying to persuade you to change your mind. In such an instance, by all means remain silent. If you say or write nothing, you are really saying that you have nothing further to say on the subject than you have already said. On no account must you send a simple acknowledgement of the letter. In certain circumstances, an acknowledgement may be taken to be agreement.

o   If the letter is long, complex, non-urgent and you are occupied with other more important things. Although your silence cannot imply agreement, it may be desirable to show that the letter will receive a reply in due course. You should reply and say just that (Fig 4.5).

o   If you are worried about the content of the letter, perhaps because it shows that you might have made a mistake or even been negligent. This is just the sort of letter that you must answer as soon as possible, otherwise, you will seem to be trying to conceal something. You need not answer by return of post – too hasty – but within a reasonable time. If you are at all doubtful, seek advice from a responsible member of the firm, a partner or the principal, not the architect on the next drawing-board.

It is important to remember that not everyone who writes to you will have great writing skills. Saying what you mean is a difficult art. If you get a letter which you do not understand, write back and say so. Ask the writer, politely, if he can rephrase his letter so that you can give it the attention it deserves (Fig 4.6).

From time to time, a contractor may write to you, asking questions, making points and suggesting claims, all in the same letter. Unless he carefully separates each item, the result can be confused. You may often know what he means although he has not said it very well. There is a great temptation to answer the letter he ought to have written rather than the letter he was written. The better way is to take each point in turn and answer it on the basis of what the contractor has clearly stated. Avoid linking items together unless your correspondent has done so himself. Always read letters carefully and answer what your correspondent has written, not what he has implied.

You will occasionally have to deal with contractors who make a habit of bombarding you with letters, maybe two or three on the same day. It is sometimes done simply to cover up the contractor's own inefficiency, sometimes to lay the groundwork for a future claim. If you are sure that the contractor is being vexatious, try to answer his letters by one-line letters, if appropriate. Do not get into the habit of devoting hours of your time to a never-ending and voluminous correspondence which can have no end product, but further dispute. The contractor may fume, but if your replies are adequate, though short, he will have nothing to complain about. Beware, however; your one-line replies will require a little thought (Fig 4.7).

4.3.4 Drafting v dictation

Unless you are possessed of a very unusual mind, you will find that it is far easier to write a good letter if you first draft it out in longhand than if you try to dictate it.

Drafting enables you to change your mind, rephrase and put sections of the letter into different orders. If you dictate, even to a secretary, you have very little chance to revise what you say. Some people try to overcome the problem by asking the secretary to type a draft letter so that it can be corrected. If the letter is complex, this can be a good idea, but to do it for every letter will make you, deservedly, unpopular unless a word processor is in use. Among the problems with dictation are:

o   Difficulty in rearranging thoughts once spoken.

Fig 4.5
'Holding' letter pending your detailed perusal


```
Dear Sir

[Heading]

Thank you for your letter of the [insert date].


[Either:]

The substance of your letter is complex and I am

anxious to give it full consideration.  The process

may take a little time, but I will reply to your

letter fully in due course.


[Or:]

In view of the complex nature of the contents I am

unable to reply immediately.  I will give careful

consideration to what you say and write to you again

shortly.


Yours faithfully
```

Fig 4.6

If you do not understand the letter

Dear Sir

[*Heading*]

Thank you for your letter of the [*insert date*].

I have read the contents several times, but unfortunately I have difficulty in understanding the precise meaning, and would prefer not to base my answer on the letter as it stands. Would you be good enough to send a rephrased version, so that I can give it proper attention.

Yours faithfully

Fig 4.7

Examples of 'one-line' replies

```
Dear Sir

[Heading]

Thank you for your letter of the [insert date], the

contents of which were answered comprehensively by

my letter of the [insert date].


[Or]

The answer to your long and involved letter of the

[insert date] is no [or yes].


[Or]

I am in receipt of your letter of the [insert date],

the contents of which do not present a true picture

of the situation.


[Or]

Thank you for your letters of the [insert dates].

My views were clearly expressed in my letter of the

[insert date].


[Or]

Thank you for your letter of the [insert date], the

answer to which is clearly shown on drawing number

[insert number].


Yours faithfully
```

o   Sentences sometimes make no sense when you see them typed out.

o   Bad style because of bad grammar and the tendency to repeat the same word.

The problems are sometimes compounded if the secretary, attempting to make sense of what you say, carries her corrections too far so that the finished letter does not quite conform with what you want to say. If the letter is urgent, you may be tempted to let it go. Resist the temptation. Once you have sent a letter, you can never retrieve it, so make sure that it conveys precisely what you intend.

This is not to say that you should never use dictation. It can be very useful if you have a multitude of short letters and Architect's Instructions to write. Simply make sure that you have a set of notes about what you wish to include. Do not throw the notes away until you have seen the finished letter. Secretaries often use their own brand of shorthand which no one else can read and they sometimes are taken ill at short notice. Dictation tapes, too, have a distressing tendency to get themselves wiped clean before they can be typed.

4.3.5 Signing

Office practice varies greatly with regard to the signing of letters. The correct way to sign letters is to sign your own name following by the typed legend 'for and on behalf of (the firm's name)'. If you merely sign your own name, you run the risk of taking personal responsibility for the contents of the letter, even though it is typed on headed stationery.

Certain contractual documents, such as Architect's Instructions, Certificates, Awards of Extensions of Time, etc., must be signed by the architect named in the contract. The person signing these documents must be an architect (unless the contract is amended to take account of an unregistered person). Therefore, before you sign, find out if you are authorised to do so.

There is a practice, which is prevalent in a number of organisations, of signing every letter with the name of the head of the department followed by the initials of the person who actually wrote the letter. Although widespread, the practice is not correct. In such cases, letters should be signed by the author followed by the legend 'for and on behalf of (the name of the head of department)'.

The use of a rubber stamp combined with initials is bad practice and meaningless.

Although it appears to be self-evidently foolhardy, architects still sometimes sign letters and other documents without reading them properly. It usually happens when the person concerned is very hard pressed; perhaps at the end of a busy day when the secretary produces a pile of papers for signature. No matter how urgent the matter or how tired you are, you should never sign anything which you have not read or you have not fully understood or with which you do not entirely agree. If you are in the slightest doubt, do not sign. Make sure that the secretary brings papers for signature at least an hour before they must go to the post. It is better to delay signing until the next morning rather than append a hasty signature.

Moreover, if you are expected to sign something produced by another person, for example a certificate based on the quantity surveyor's figures, be sure that you understand his calculations. Do not hesitate to seek further information in such cases. Remember, if you sign, you take responsibility.

4.3.6 Standard letters

The use of standard letters for standard situations (see Appendix A) is a good idea for saving time. Ensure that a copy of the standard letter goes onto the file in question. Extreme care should be taken in the use of standard letters because what appears to be a standard situation may, in fact, have subtle variations from the norm: which may indicate the use of a purpose-written letter in that particular case.

In particular, beware of using standard acknowledgement letters (see section 4.3.3). They may imply that you agree with your correspondent. Compliments slips should be banned. They are not only useless, they are positively dangerous because they give no record of what they enclose. It is very tempting to send the odd copy letter or drawing with a compliments slip when you are busy, but if you do so you retain no record of what you sent, or to whom and when. Theoretically, drawing registers are kept, but they are essentially in-house records. They are not always kept up to date. Everything going out of the office should have a letter attached stating what you are enclosing. You may think that you are saving time by using a compliments slip, but it is just those items sent out when you are busy which will return to haunt you in the future. If the contractor later denies that he ever received information sent under cover of a compliments slip, you have no means of showing that you ever sent it. A carbon copy of a letter, on the other hand, is generally good evidence that the original letter was sent.

4.3.7 General points

o   Never use forenames in business letters (e.g., 'Dear Fred') unless you are dealing with a client who is, or becomes, a friend. It suggests a friendliness which is purely artificial.

o   Avoid business letter shorthand, e.g., 'ult.', 'inst.'.

o   Leaving the recipient with a dignified way out of his difficulty will avoid many disputes.

o   Always leave yourself room to manœuvre.

o   When writing about a contractual matter, wherever possible use the exact wording in the contract. It makes clear that you are acting in accordance with the contact.

o   Reply to reasonable letters reasonably. Reply to unreasonable letters reasonably.

o   You may be justified in writing an angry letter, but it may not look good in an arbitration.

o   Always write your letters as though they will be read out in court; they may be, one day.

4.4   Reports

4.4.1   Introduction

You should try to keep your letters to one A4 sheet. If you need to write more than two sheets, consider whether it would not be better to produce a report. A report is a formal document. It is usually produced after investigation or consideration of some problem or event. If you are asked to produce a report for any reason, it is important to remember that a rambling note will not suffice. A report should be structured. If the architect co-ordinating your team asks you to report to him about some aspect of the work, it may simply mean that he wants you to give him an oral report. At the most he will expect no more than a few brief notes, probably numbered in sequence.

The most important reports you will be called upon to write, however, are intended for clients. Little instruction is given on report writing and it is common to simply unearth an old report on a similar topic and use it as a guide. This is only partially helpful and it may be better to develop your report format from basic principles.

An efficient office will have a number of different report formats, complete with checklists, to enable reports to be produced quickly without omitting essential details. There are many books on the subject of report writing in general and one on report writing for architects (see Appendix A) which should prove helpful.

4.4.2   Subjects

There are a number of common subjects which might be expected to generate reports from time to time. They are as follows:

o   Feasibility.

o   Outline proposals.
o   Scheme design.
o   Progress reports.
o   Special reports on some aspect of a project or contract.
o   Report on claim for loss and/or expense.
o   Report on grant of extension of time.
o   General development possibilities for land or buildings.
o   Inspection of property.
o   Schedule of condition.
o   Investigation of defects.
o   Ecclesiastical property report.

A few words about the purpose of each report should be helpful:

Feasibility

This type of report is produced as part of stage B of the RIBA Plan of Work. After the brief has been taken, it is usual to produce such a report for the client so that he can decide whether to proceed with the project. For this purpose a very full package of information must be assembled including all the data necessary for the client to make a decision. If in doubt, more, rather than less, information should be included. The actual amount of information will vary, of course, depending on the size of the project, but it is essential to include the cost implications of different approaches to the work.

Outline proposals

On small works, this type of report is often combined with the feasibility report. It is produced as part of stage C of the RIBA Plan of Work. The purpose is to explain the thinking behind the initial design.

Scheme design

Part of stage D of the RIBA Plan of Work. Similar to the outline proposal report, but more detailed as work on the project is more advanced. There is no necessity for both types of report if the works are minor.

Progress reports

This type of report is sent to the client to inform him of the state of the job during operations on site. It is useful to number the reports consecutively so that any item can be found in any report simply by reference to its number. It should be sent to the client after each site meeting. Do not simply send a copy of the minutes of the site meetings. They contain information the client does not require and omit information he needs.

Special reports on some aspect of a project or contract

The need to produce such a report will be rare. Difficult problems requiring the client's decision will be covered. Such things might be the possibility of determining the contractor's employment or a claim by third parties.

Report on a claim for loss and/or expense
Although it is your duty to decide the validity of contractor's claims, it is advisable to keep the client informed so that he can plan ahead for any unforeseen financial commitment he may acquire.

Report on grant of extension of time
It is your duty to decide extensions of time, but it is sensible to keep the client informed of the main points of the contractor's claim and your decision.

Development possibilities for land or buildings
This is the kind of report which can prove important in determining whether a large project should proceed. Although similar to a feasibility report, you will often be expected to present alternative suggestions for the consideration of your client. For example, your client may have to decide whether it would be better to develop a site for offices, shops or entertainment use. Your report will form the key factor in his deliberations, but beware of venturing beyond your own field of expertise.

Inspection of property
This type of report is usually prepared before property is purchased. You will be expected to produce a detailed report including such things as dimensions of rooms, fixed furniture, state of repair and structural condition. Attention must also be paid to the surroundings and the effect of any planning permission.

Schedule of condition
Usually carried out before building operations when it is essential to record the precise condition of the building so that the effect of the work can be determined afterwards or before the commencement of a lease. It should be differentiated from a schedule for dilapidation which is carried out during the term of a lease to ensure that the tenant is carrying out his obligations, before termination of lease to ensure that all repairs have been done or after termination for the same purpose. It is important to secure the agreement of all interested parties. Failing such agreement, you must rely on your own professional judgment. Although these reports have similarities to property inspections, you must always bear in mind the purpose for which the report is required. For example, a schedule of condition before underpinning should record every crack no matter how small and you might recommend the fitting of tell-tales.

Investigation of defects

This is a specialised type of report which you should not attempt unless you have the appropriate skill and experience. It is highly likely that your report will be used in court at some stage and you will be closely questioned on its contents. You will be expected to state the facts, give your opinion as to the cause and suggest suitable means of rectifying the trouble.

Ecclesiastical property report

Another specialised type of report. Very often the ecclesiastical authorities will supply a special report format which they require you to follow. It is usual to carry out ecclesiastical inspections at regular intervals, commonly every five or six years. It is similar to a property inspection, but you will possibly be required to give your opinion on the worth of various items in the building. Do not attempt this type of report unless you have considerable experience and knowledge of the subject.

Fig 4.8

Normally accepted structure of a book

- Title page
- Preface
- Table of contents
- List of illustrations
- Acknowledgements
- Introduction
- Text
- Bibliography
- Appendices
- Index

Fig 4.9

Structure for a report

- Title page
- Table of contents
- Introduction
- Summary (if required)
- Text
- Appendices (can include acknowledgements and bibliography)

4.4.3 Important points to note

o   Do not write a report if a short letter will do the same job, but do not write a long complicated letter if you can make your points clearer in a report.

o   Remember your reader. He will usually be a layman. Do not use technical terms which may prove difficult to understand. If you are writing for the benefit of a fellow professional, you should make full use of technical terms which will shorten your report.

o   Never use jargon.

o   Use a published format or make your own before you begin to write. It makes the act of marshalling your thoughts so much easier because it compartments them.

o   The report should follow a recognised structure. The generally accepted structure for all types of books is shown in Fig 4.8. Reports do not usually warrant such elaboration and the structure shown in Fig 4.9 is usually sufficient.

o   The presentation is almost as important as the report itself because if it is badly presented, it will not be read. Leave good margins. Number pages and paragraphs clearly so as to assist in the locating of specific portions of the report. Avoid separate notes and references if possible; they should form part of the appendices. Large sheets, such as plans, should be put at the back and should be folded so that they can be easily referred to. The finished report should be so bound that it can be opened flat.

o   Divide your report into fact and opinion and make the distinction clear. Your opinions should follow naturally from the facts. Therefore, put the facts first.

o   End your report with a question or a series of questions to ensure that there is a follow up.

o   If the report is long, you may find it convenient to put a summary of the main points at the beginning.

o   Avoid excessive cross-referencing.

o   Be brief and to the point at all times.

o   The inclusion of the occasional afterthought in a letter may be tolerated; never in a report. Do not hesitate to draft and redraft a report until you get it right.

4.5   Meetings

4.5.1   Purpose

You will be involved in a large number of meetings during your career.

Sometimes you will organise them for your own purposes, at other times you will simply be required to attend to contribute information and opinions. There are two basic types of meeting;

O   Planned or formal.

O   Unplanned or informal.

Unplanned meetings take place whenever you have to discuss anything with one or more than one other person. Generally, unplanned meetings do not concern us in this chapter.

Most people dislike meetings because it is felt that they:

O   Waste time.

O   Achieve little.

There are, of course, some people who actually enjoy meetings because they have a sense of achievement by the mere fact of attending or because they enjoy the status of chairman or simply because they like the opportunity to talk while others listen. These people sometimes attend meetings because they have very little to occupy their time. If you have not already done so, you will learn to recognise them. Avoid attending their meetings if at all possible.

The purpose of a meeting may be to exchange information or to solve a problem. Meetings can consist of just two or three people or as many as thirty. Although a very large meeting, if well run, can usefully function to exchange information, problem solving is more successful the fewer the number who are present. The difficulty with a large meeting, besides the multitudes of opinions, is that everyone is keen to contribute and discussion can be never ending. This is why, in every walk of life, large committees appoint some of their members to form sub-committees to formulate and present positive suggestions.

If you are thinking of calling a meeting, the most important thing you can do is to stop and decide whether the meeting is really necessary. Too many meetings simply perpetuate themselves long after the original reason for the meeting has vanished. Phrases such as 'These get-togethers are a really good forum for the exchange of ideas' suggest that the meeting is obsolete. If you are appointed to a new post, you will often find that you have inherited attendance at a number of regular meetings. Look at each one critically and if you decide that it is achieving nothing, or what little it is achieving could be accomplished more efficiently by other means, do not hesitate to say so. If you do not, sooner or later someone else will. Even excluding those people who seem to spend their whole lives attending meetings, there are many people who welcome a meeting as a break from dull routine and they will strongly oppose any suggestion that regular meetings should be stopped. If you cannot put an end to any particular regular meeting which is achieving nothing, try to excuse yourself from attending. Do not hesitate to suggest a colleague as better fitted for the duty, he may have nothing better to do with his time – you have. If you decide that you have to call a meeting, the next thing to do is to decide the maximum number of people it is necessary to invite. The fewer the better. Make sure that the people you invite are competent to make the decisions required. In general, these people will be the most senior and, therefore, the busiest. They will be anxious to get away, and therefore, decision making should be rapid and general chat reduced.

4.5.2 Types

The meetings which you might call can be roughly divided into five groups:
- Staff meetings.
- Client meetings.
- Design team meetings.
- Site meetings.
- Meetings for special purposes.

Staff meetings
This type of meeting is usually initiated by a principal or partner, but possibly also by an associate or senior member of staff, which could be you. The purpose might be to discuss pensions, discipline, office reorganisation or workload, etc. If you are asked to attend, there is no real way you can avoid it. Indeed, you should not try to avoid it because staff meetings are never called without some express purpose in mind. If you are in a position to call such a meeting yourself, only do so if you cannot achieve the same objective by speaking to colleagues individually. Meetings rarely save time.

Client meetings
Sometimes, this type of meeting is called by the client. More often, you will initiate it for the purpose of presenting proposals or obtaining decisions or both. Ideally, the meeting will be between you and your client alone. It is sometimes advantageous, however, to have other people present to ensure that decisions are not delayed; such people as solicitors, estate agents and quantity surveyors can be useful in this respect. Do not get into the habit of inviting such people without first considering whether it is likely that they will be needed; it is expensive and time-wasting. Your client may well be a committee or board of directors in which case, the fewer additional people you invite the quicker the meeting will be over.

Design team meetings
There is no way that you can avoid this type of meeting. If the project is of any size, the numbers present at the meetings could include the client, all

consultants, some of your colleagues and, possibly, the contractor. Although this is a necessary meeting, you can restrict the frequency by calling such meetings only at key points in the development of the scheme. The habit of calling regular meetings of the design team just to find out if everything is on schedule is counter-productive. You should have one meeting at the very beginning of the project when everyone can exchange ideas and information, one after the scheme has been prepared and another during the preparation of production information. In between, you may find it more efficient to discuss the scheme individually with the members concerned.

Site meetings
Much rubbish has been written about the necessity for site meetings. Clearly, it is not conceivable that you will be able to complete a contract without the necessity of some meetings to discuss special problems, but regular fortnightly or monthly site meetings have little to commend them. The practice is deeply entrenched in the building industry, however, and you may be thought careless if you do not conform.

What does a site meeting seek to achieve? The answer seems to be one or more of the following:

o   Measure actual against predicted progress.
o   Answer queries.
o   Provide information.

Your only positive role in assisting progress is to make sure that you supply all necessary information at the correct time. Progress, itself, is in the hands of the contractor whose best interests will be served by a quick and workmanlike conclusion to the contract. The clerk of works will send you a weekly progress report, the contractor can be asked to do the same; sometimes he does that anyway. Any problems with regard to progress can most readily be taken up directly between you and the contractor by telephone or, better, in correspondence.

Since most queries inevitably crop up between site meetings, they are not really a forum for answering them. Very few queries are incapable of being dealt with by telephone, letter or drawing. Site meetings are invariably preceded or followed by a site inspection. You can inspect without having a meeting.

Provision of information is best done by correspondence, thus ensuring that you have a proper record of what you send.

Attendance at site meetings usually consists of the architect and another member of staff to take minutes, one or more representatives of the contractor's head office including the contractor's surveyor, the person-in-charge, the clerk of works, the quantity surveyor, any other consultant and possibly a representative from some other organisation or firm with an interest in being present. Site meetings can take many hours of everyone's time. Most of the time is taken up by discussing progress and fruitless argument. Many of the participants will have little to contribute. Think carefully before you embark on regular time-wasting exercises of this sort. One type of meeting it is essential to have will be the first meeting before the work starts on site (often erroneously called the 'pre-contract meeting'). Everyone connected with the contract should be present and it gives the opportunity for all parties to get to know one another. It also gives you the opportunity to emphasise important aspects of the project so as to leave no one in doubt.

Meetings for special purposes
This type of meeting has to be arranged from time to time to settle important points with regard to planning or ministry submissions or the like. The golden rule is to be prepared and involve as few people as possible.

4.5.3 Preparation

Preparing for a meeting is as important as the meeting itself, otherwise nothing will be achieved. Assuming that you have decided that a meeting must be arranged, you must clearly set down the purpose or purposes of the meeting. It is usual to prepare an agenda and attach any useful information for the attention of the participants. Always circulate the agenda and information a week before any meeting to give people time to carry out their research.

Although there is a generally agreed standard format for most meetings (see Fig 4.10), you are advised to produce your own individual agenda to suit yourself. Do not simply list the items. Explain what will be required of the meeting. An example of such an agenda produced for a meeting with the client is shown in Fig 4.11. Give some consideration to the structure of the agenda. For example, you may think that it is better to begin with all the non-contentious items of minor importance, so that they can be disposed of before discussion of the main item begins, but beware that it is always difficult to predict which will be the contentious items. You may find that the meeting exhausts itself on minor points, leaving little enthusiasm for the really important topics. Some suggested structures are show in Figs 4.12 and 4.13, but remember that each meeting must be assessed separately.

Another important matter is to consider how the participants' time will be occupied. For example, if one party will be concerned with only two items, it may be better to get him out of the way early, or schedule him for the end so that he knows precisely when he will be required.

The whole question of time is crucially important. Naturally, meetings should be arranged at times which are convenient for the participants.

The times should not be too convenient, however. Particularly avoid having a meeting after lunch. Many people find it difficult to concentrate at this time and one or two may actually fall asleep. Some architects arrange to have their most important meetings on Friday afternoons. The reasoning seems to be that such a time will ensure that the meeting does not overrun. On the other hand, you will find that quite a few people treat Friday afternoon as a sort of end of term and this, combined with a heavy lunch, may frustrate your good intentions. The best time is probably the end of the morning. Most people are at their best then and a meeting timed to begin at 11.30 am will get through its business rapidly and efficiently if the participants know that they will not be released until it is completed.

Do avoid so-called 'working lunches'. Unless you know it is going to be a pleasant discussion over a good meal with just two or three others, you are wasting valuable relaxation time. The working lunch is a most uncivilised invention of those who like to think that every minute of their time is spent busily working. The principal outcome of most such meetings is indigestion. If you make it clear that you will not send out for sandwiches if the meeting runs into the lunch break, the meeting is much more likely to finish promptly.

Assign time periods for each item on the agenda and an overall time for the meeting as a whole. Show the times on the agenda which you circulate. Long meetings are very tiring. It is better to have two meetings on separate days lasting an hour each than one long meeting lasting three hours.

4.5.4 The meeting

If you are chairing the meeting, it is your job to control the proceedings. This is not an easy task. You must make sure that the meeting begins promptly at the time stated, deals with the items adequately and ends on time. If you build up a reputation as a good chairman, successive meet-

---

Fig 4.10
Generally accepted standard format for meetings

---

1. Record of those present including status.
2. Apologies for absence.
3. Agreement to minutes of last meeting (if any).
4. Matters arising from the minutes of the last meeting (if any).
5. Items.
6. Any other buisiness.
7. Date and time of next meeting (if any).

Fig 4.11

Example of agenda for meeting with client

Meeting between Wren Pugin & Jones Associates, Architects

William Raites, Quantity Surveyor, and

Vherrie Lharge Developments Ltd., Client

Re: Proposed Warehouse, Beezee Industrial Estate,

   Bradfield, East Yorkshire.

Date: 2nd August 1985, Commencing: 11.00 am

                         Concluding: 12.15 pm

AGENDA

1. Finance: Consider latest cost plan and consider

    the necessity to make reductions (cost plan

    attached)

    (15 minutes)

2. Design: Consider architects' report of 1st July

    1985 and make decisions relating to:

    2.1   Phasing

    2.2   Cladding

    2.3   Landscaping provision

    (30 minutes)

3. Timing: Make final decisions regarding dates

    for:

    3.1   Invitation to tender

    3.2   Possession

    3.3   Completion

    (15 minutes)

4. Logo: Determine means of incorporation.

    (10 minutes)

Fig 4.12

Suggested agenda structure A

Apologies

Agreement to minutes of previous meeting (if any)

Matters arising (allow 5 minutes total)

Minor items which must be decided first (allow 5

minutes each)

Major items ⎤

Reports ⎬ Core

Decisions ⎦

Minor items which can be deferred if necessary

(allow 5 minutes each)

Fig 4.13

Suggested agenda structure B

```
Apologies

Agreement to minutes of previous meeting (if any)

Matters arising (allow 5 minutes total)

Major items   ⎤
Reports       ⎬        Core
Decisions     ⎦


Minor items requiring a decision immediately (allow
5 minutes each)


Minor items which can be deferred if necessary
(allow 5 minutes each)
```

ings will become easier. As chairman, it is not enough for you to announce the item and wait hopefully for someone to begin. You should introduce each topic. You need not be impartial. If you know that a certain person has something to contribute, do not wait, ask him to speak. Be ready to cut off those people who are simply wasting time. Do not try to be popular, try to be effective. If the topic is particularly complicated, be ready at the outset with suggestions to perhaps break it down into manageable parts. It is inevitable that some members will fail to grasp the point and they can, if unchecked, ramble on at length. It is part of your job to see when this is happening and to step in firmly to put the meeting back on course. From time to time, you will come across the person who tries to use the meeting as a platform for his grievances, possibly quite unrelated to the subject under discussion. Do not allow such a person to continue. If necessary ask him to leave suggesting that he put his points to you in writing. Above all, you must be single-minded. Always remember the purpose of the meeting and concentrate on achieving it.

After every item, make sure that everyone is agreed on what has been decided. Too many meetings fail in their purpose because some of the participants misunderstand what has been agreed; they complain when they see the minutes and you may have to arrange another meeting to go over the items again. If time is running short, omit minor items and proceed directly to the major issues. The same principle holds good if discussion is becoming protracted on some item you imagined would cause no problems. In such a case, simply refer the item back for discussion at some future date and close the dicussion on that particular point. Do it firmly and do not tolerate any last thoughts from anyone.

Minutes should be brief. Although it can be distracting to take them yourself if you are acting as chairman, you must always be in control of what is written. Either dictate the minute to a secretary at the end of each item or make a brief note yourself. In either case, be prepared to spend some time drafting the minutes after the meeting is ended. The most important part of the minutes is the decision reached on each item. The arguments for and against, which preceded the decision, may be entertaining or revealing, but they have no place in the minutes. Time is valuable. If the minutes are clearly set out and concise, there is much more chance that they will be read and acted upon than if they are long and involved. The ideal is to aim to confine minutes to one side of a sheet of A4 paper. Opinions differ regarding the wisdom of incorporating an 'action column' in the minutes. It certainly makes it easy to identify a particular action as being the responsibility of a particular person, but the danger is that the person concerned will get into the habit of reading only the action column, not the actual decisions. Also, if a mistake is made, no one may take the action.

In order to reduce the minutes, it is useful to have a front sheet containing basic information and put the decisions on a separate sheet fastened to the back. An example of a typical front sheet is shown in Fig 4.14. The device is particularly useful if a series of meetings (such as site meetings!) are to be held. Most of the information on the front sheet can be standardised for each meeting.

Ideally, minutes should be prepared immediately after the meeting and distributed forthwith. If this is impossible, ensure that distribution occurs within twenty-four hours so that the minutes are received while the participants are still clear about the points discussed. If you leave it until the following week, memories will be dimmer and queries will multiply. The distribution list should be on the minutes so that everyone knows who has a copy. Everyone who attends the meeting should have a copy of the minutes, together with anyone else who has an interest in any of the items. Two suggestions:

o   Do not send copies to people or organisations unless you really think it is necessary. Too often, minutes are distributed without any real thought and most people have quite enough paper to deal with already.

o   If the recipient is only interested in one particular item, it may be better to send a brief letter instead quoting the minute (Fig 4.15).

When you receive minutes of a meeting you have attended, read them immediately. If there is anything which you think is wrong or with which you disagree, write immediately and make your point. Even if the meeting is one of a series, do not wait until the next meeting to record your disagreement. If the point is of vital importance, send copies of your letter to everyone circulated with the original minutes. (Fig 4.16).

It is important to remember that minutes have no real standing as a true record of the matters they contain unless there is a subsequent recorded agreement. Agreement can never be implied by silence. The issue of certificates, notices or instructions cannot be done by recording them in minutes. You must separately issue such certificates, etc., in the ordinary way. The same holds true of any notices or applications which the contract requires the contractor to make.

If you have to attend a meeting called by someone else, you may find that it is badly prepared and badly controlled. Do not hesitate to speak and act firmly, at least to those items with which you are particularly concerned. If the chairman is weak, it is relatively easy for a determined participant to effectively take control. You will often find other members only too willing to allow you to take the lead. But in such cases, read the minutes carefully.

Fig 4.14

Typical cover sheet for minutes

Job title:	Meeting no:
Job number:	
Location:	Date:
	Time:

Present:

Apologies:

Date and time of next meeting:

Circulation:

Employer	copies	Mech. Eng.	copies
Contractor	copies	Elect. Eng.	copies
Quant. Surv.	copies	Lscp. Archt.	copies
Struct. Eng.	copies	Clerk of Wks.	copies
Heat. & Vent. Eng.	copies	File	copies

Wren Pugin and Jones Associates

Architects

Gothic Chambers

Brum   Tel: (0101) 10101

4.6 Time-sheets

4.6.1 Introduction

Most, but surprisingly not all, offices use time-sheets. Their purpose is twofold:

o   To provide data for the charging of fees on a time basis.

o   To provide a means for assessing performance standards within an office in relation to various projects.

The *Architect's Appointment*, clause 4.15, commits the architect to maintaining records of time spent on services performed on a time basis. These records must be produced to the client on request. Even without this stipulation, it is difficult to see how a time charge could be made without time-sheets.

Unless the means is available for an office to monitor its progress in a methodical way and assess performance at the end of a job, job planning remains pure guesswork.

4.6.2 The system

Although practice varies, the filling in of time-sheets is usually restricted to technical staff, secretarial and typing costs being lumped in with overheads. The reason for this is really practical. A telephonist, receptionist or secretary cannot easily split her time into jobs. For the same reason, principals and partners rarely fill complete time-sheets for the whole of their time. Of course partners must keep a record of their time if it is intended to charge a client on this basis and, indeed, it is good practice for partners to keep proper time-sheets in order properly to check how time is allocated against each job.

Most offices have their own ideas about the layout of time-sheets, but suggested headings are shown in Fig 4.17. It is a good idea to include a column for expenses even though the expenses incurred in connection with a particular job can be extracted from expense claims. Time-sheets should be clear and concise. Although every office will have its own system of recording time and costing, a typical procedure is as follows:

Time-sheets are collected on Monday morning. Whoever is responsible for doing so then collates all the hours (and expenses too if included) on a master sheet for each job. If the hours are then costed out, it is possible to see whether the job is financially on target, from an office point of view. In some offices, a graph is drawn to show the relationship between forecast and actual expenditure. It is, of course, possible to draw the graph purely in hourly terms, but since members of staff are paid at different rates, a false picture can emerge. Time charges to the client become simply a mat-

Fig 4.15
Enclosing extract of minutes

Dear Sir

[*Heading*]

At a meeting held on the [*insert date*] between
[*insert names of principal participants*], it was
resolved as follows:

    [*insert minute, including reference number*]

[*Then, either:*]

I should be pleased if you would take whatever
action you think appropriate.

[*Or:*]

I should be pleased to receive your comments.

[*Or:*]

I should be pleased if you would note the minute as
appropriate.

Yours faithfully

Fig 4.16

If you disagree with minutes you have received

```
Dear Sir

[Heading]

I have examined the minutes of the meeting held on

the [insert date] which I received today.  I have

the following comments to make:

    [insert list of comments]


Please arrange to have these comments published at

the next meeting and inserted in the appropriate

place in the minutes.


Yours faithfully



Copies: [To all those present at the meeting and

        included in the circulation list.]
```

Fig 4.17

Time-sheet headings

Date	Job No.	Job	RIBA work stage	Hours	Expenses

Fig 4.18

Example of completed time-sheet

Date	Job No.	Job	RIBA work stage	Hours	Expenses
2.8.85	1306	OK offices	F	$3^{30}/_{60}$	
"	759	Conlon House	K	$1^{30}/_{60}$	4 miles @ 30p
"	942	Richardsons Entertainments	K	$^{10}/_{60}$	
"	1363	Elliott Housing Estate	B	$^{10}/_{60}$	
"	641	Farour MDC	Defects Research	1	
"	1400	Rawson House	A	$^{5}/_{60}$	
"	1306	Sandham Engineering	F	$_{\sim}1$	
3.8.85					

ter of extracting the hours for each member of staff and multiplying by the appropriate factor in each case.

It is clear that accurate filling in of time-sheets is intimately related to the financial accounting of the office and, ultimately, to its success or failure.

4.6.3 You and your time-sheet

Never make the mistake of thinking that it does not matter whether you fill in your time-sheet accurately. It is common for architects to be lax in filling in time-sheets. After all, it is not considered to be a very creative occupation. For this reason, time-sheets are often left until last thing on Friday afternoon, when much frantic wracking of brains results in fiction being written down. Little guidance is given about time-sheets. The fact is that they are not always easy to complete. Your time-sheet should be left at the side of your drawing-board. Do not even leave its completion until the end of the day, fill it in as you go through the day. Get into the habit and it becomes easy. Most solicitors work in this way and there could be a lesson in that!

If you are working on one project, your time-sheet will be easy to complete. But do not forget the numerous telephone calls which you might receive or make during the time you are working on your main project. It is easy to ignore a single five-minute call, but you may have ten five-minute calls in one day. The answer is to log every time you change from one job to another. Five minutes is the smallest unit it is reasonable to log down and longer periods should be in multiples. Completing your time-sheet at the end of the day means that you will forget most of the small periods of time and, if the main project is charged on a time basis, your client may be paying more than he should. Do not become overly scrupulous about your time-sheet, however. Use common sense.

Prompt and accurate feedback to the architects responsible for each project is an indispensable part of the system. If it can be seen, at an early stage, that the allocated time will overrun, steps can be taken to deal with it. If you find that your project is swallowing up more time than expected, by all means try to recover the situation. But do not start allocating your time to other things in order to make the paper result look good. To do so is completely to destroy the point of time-sheets. The reason why you are overrunning could be because the original estimate of time was low or because the client changed his mind at an important stage and should be charged extra fees. If you fake your time-sheets, you are making nonsense of the office records on which future estimates will be made.

Fig 4.18 is an example of a time-sheet filled in for one day by an architect who is dealing with several projects, one of which is on the drawing-board.

4.7 Filing

4.7.1 Types

Every architectural office is faced with the problem of what to do with the enormous amount of paper generated by internal and external forces. Most of it has to be kept, at least for a limited period, and during the time it is kept, it must be accessible. Office filing systems can be divided into five categories:

o   Drawings.
o   Job files.
o   Special files.
o   Management files.
o   Technical literature and books.

Drawings
Within this category, it is possible to subdivide further into:
o   Current drawings.
o   Drawings which are no longer current, but not 'dead'.
o   'Dead' drawings which are not generally a source of reference.
Current drawings are all those drawings which relate to projects which are in one of the RIBA Work Stages. They are in constant use and should be filed in the drawing office. Every office varies in choice of method of storage. The important thing is that you should get to know the system as a priority matter. This is particularly important if you are in a senior position and perhaps not on the drawing-board regularly. It is too easy to ask someone else to get a drawing for you. One day you may find that you need to consult a drawing and there is no one to find it for you. All current drawings should be filed immediately they are completed and drawings should not be left around the office if they are not required for reference at the moment. Get into the habit of putting your drawings away promptly. 'Dead' drawings are usually filed away from the drawing office, sometimes in a basement. It is a matter of choice whether such drawings are kept in their original state or microfilmed. Microfilms occupy very little space and can be referred to easily with the aid of a reader. On the other hand, reproduction can be a problem and it is more expensive than taking an ordinary print from a negative. Some offices have all their dead drawings microfilmed as a matter of course, some only microfilm the principal drawings in each set. Other offices do not save any drawings at all after a period of six or twelve years from the issue of the final certificate depending upon whether the contract was under hand or under seal respectively. It should be noted, however, that drawings and the appropriate correspondence file are the property of the client and the correct

procedure at the end of a job is to ask him if he wants you to deliver all such material to him. Since it is clear that the liability of an office can extend far into the future, the decision is one which will be taken by the partners. The basic rule seems to be that the office should save everything or nothing. To take a middle course is pointless.

Drawings which are not current but not yet dead should ideally be stored in a special file. More often they are kept in the drawing office with the current drawings. Such drawings may be schemes which have been prepared, but are not proceeded with until the client's finances improve: e.g. production drawings for a project which has been completed, but which it is expected will be extended in the near future.

Job files

They are usually kept so as to be convenient for the secretarial staff, who are responsible for keeping them in order. Ideally, they should also be convenient for the technical staff. Avoid the habit of keeping stacks of job files on your desk. Usually, you will only need one at once. It is annoying and time wasting to have to enquire throughout the office to find a particular file.

Special files

These may be files on such subjects as fee negotiations, correspondence with solicitors and leases, etc. They are not usually kept with the job files, but in one of the partners' offices. They are not normally accessible to anyone except partners, private secretaries and, possibly, those of the senior staff who need to use them.

Management files

Like special files, they are accessible only to partners and private secretaries. They cover such subjects as staff data and salaries, accounts, partnership meetings and expenses.

Technical literature and books

This type of file is usually termed the office library. Its size and scope depends upon the office. All technical literature should be kept together although, in many cases, every member of the technical staff has a small private library of favourite literature and useful books. This is not entirely a bad thing, but avoid duplicating information which is already in the office library. Most libraries are filed under the CI/SfB system now and there are a number of systems on the market which include an updating service on a regular basis. Every architect should know how to use the library as an essential tool of his profession.

4.7.2 General points

○ Every incoming letter is seen by a partner. Often it is stamped with a little box in which he can indicate who is to deal with it. Try to ensure that you deal with all mail on the same day you receive it. If it is impossible to do this, send it to file and operate the 'bring forward' procedure (see section 7.1.3). Try to gain a reputation for having a clear desk as far as mail is concerned. It will enhance your overall efficient image.

○ It is useful for all members of staff to have the opportunity to see letters sent out by their colleagues. Too often, the first intimation you have that a partner has written a letter concerning your job is when you discover it on file. It is inefficient, it is indefensible, but it does happen. The only way to make sure that everyone knows what everyone else is doing is to circulate copies of all outgoing mail each day. Depending upon the size of the practice, it may be done on an office or group basis. The copies should be pinned in a folder with a circulation list on the cover. One of the administrative staff should be responsible for it and see that it circulates quickly. If your office does not operate such a system, suggest it. There will be those who lament that they already have too much paper to read. They can simply initial the circulation list and pass on the folder if they so wish. Be sure that you read it thoroughly. If you do, you can become, in a few months, the only person who has a good overall view of the work the office is doing. Partners' confidential letters will not be included in the folder.

○ Make sure that the drawing and correspondence files for your jobs are in good order; you never know when you may need to find something in a hurry.

4.8   Reproduction

4.8.1 Drawings

Every office has to have drawings reproduced. The system of accomplishing this varies from office to office and in different parts of the country.

Many offices send their drawings, on a daily basis, to a central agency which undertakes all types of reproduction. This is especially popular in London. A great many offices, however, rely upon their own equipment to produce copies of drawings. If you are employed in an office which favours sending drawings to a central agency, you should have few problems. What follows assumes that your office operates its own system.

There are numerous methods of drawing reproduction. Your office will have one of them. Unless the system is really poor, you have no chance of altering it.

If the office is large enough, prints will be produced by someone who does very little else. More often, prints are the responsibility of the lowest paid member of staff who will have other duties to fill the rest of his time. Whoever is responsible, get to know him and treat him well. The day will come when you need prints producing urgently and you will get priority if the print man knows you appreciate his service.

If you are in a hurry, you may be tempted to do the printing yourself. If there is really no one else who can do the job, you may have no option. Do find out as soon as you join the office, how to work the print machine, but do not fall into the trap of being the only person, other than the print man, who can do it. If, in the print man's absence, a colleague asks you to take some prints for him, insist on showing him how to do it, then leave him to get on with it.

Spend a couple of hours finding out exactly what the print machine will do. Note its strengths and, particularly, its weaknesses. Then you will know whether to send any important drawings to an outside firm for reproduction without wasting time with the office machine.

Microfilmed drawings can be reproduced in the office, if you have a printer, otherwise you will have to send them to a firm which specialises in the work. The quality of such reproductions varies considerably so, before sending the microfilm, always check that the firm can reproduce to the standard you require.

4.8.2 Other documents

No office is without a copying machine for A4 and sometimes A3 documents. A useful refinement is the ability to enlarge or reduce documents. Many offices use standard A4 and A3 details which are conveniently copied using a standard copier. A point to watch, however, is the scale. Some machines often produce a copy which is slightly reduced from the original. This need not concern you unduly provided that you fully dimension your drawings and draw a scale on the drawing.

4.8.3 General points

o   It is useful too have contacts with other drawing offices in the locality. They can often provide help in reproducing drawings if you have a problem. Your contact need not be on an official basis, indeed you will often find it easier to get things done through the good offices of a friend. Be ready to reciprocate.

o   Be economical. Always choose the cheapest acceptable method of reproduction.

4.9   Working for a contractor

4.9.1 Capacity and status

If you are employed in the contractor's organisation, you will probably be working in one or both of the following capacities.

o   An architect carrying out the normal functions.

o   An architect carrying out functions associated with contracting.

In the first case, you will usually work in an office, probably with other architects, and you will behave much as you would if you were in private practice, receiving the brief from the contractor's client, preparing feasibility studies and sketch schemes, production drawings, etc. You will not, of course, be involved in tendering except, perhaps, in the case of sub-contractors. After you have produced the working drawings, probably in consultation with the contracts manager, they will go to the estimating department for quantities and pricing.

If you are carrying out functions associated with contracting, you may not produce any drawings at all. You are likely to be involved in checking drawings received from other architects and sub-contractors, quality control on site and the giving of contract advice. Your duties may mean that you attend site meetings, handle correspondence, prepare claims and generally look out for the contractor's interests. It is impossible to be specific because, if you choose this kind of work, your assistance will usually be welcomed in most aspects of the contractor's business. It can be an interesting and rewarding activity, especially now that there is no bar on you eventually becoming a director of the firm. You may allow the contractor to use your name on his letterhead as staff architect.

4.9.2 Objectives

The contractor's objective is to produce a building which is adequate in relation to his express or implied obligations under the contract and in so doing to make an acceptable profit. Additionally, he wants to satisfy the client. This is a perfectly good set of principles as far as the contractor is concerned. It is important that you keep these principles before you at all times. Few contractors are rogues. If you find that you are working for a rogue, move. Staying on will frustrate you and do you no good. You may be surprised to find that most contractors have as good a set of ethics as you have yourself and they will never expect you to act against your professional judgment. Indeed, that is probably why they appointed you in the first place. Most contractors are very practical people, interested in straightforward solutions to problems. They will not expect you to agonise over abstruse design theory.

4.9.3 Relations with third parties

If you are employed by a contractor, you cannot give the client independent advice. Principle 2.3 of the *RIBA Code of Professional Conduct* lays
down very clear rules:
'A member shall not and shall not purport to carry out the independent
functions of an architect or of a supervising officer in relation to a contract
in which he or his employer is the contractor.' The note to this rule states;
'Where the client of a member providing a contracting service requires
independent advice on quality and budgetary control the member should
inform the client of this right to appoint another architect to act as his
professional adviser and agent.'
The principle is important because many clients will not realise that there
is any difference between you and an independent architect. You must
interpret the spirit of the rule. It is for you to decide when it is clear that
the client is asking your advice as though you were independent. Clearly,
you may have problems with your employer, the contractor, who may not
relish the fact that you are advising the client to look elsewhere for advice.
One way to solve this difficulty is to make the contrator aware, when you
accept the post, that you are still governed by a strict code of conduct. If
the contractor is agreeable, you could arrange that each client receives a
standard letter (Fig 4.19) setting out the position tactfully. Remember
that, whether the contractor sees your point of view or not, it does not alter
your professional position. The value of sending such a letter to the client
lies in the fact that, by the letter, you have discharged that responsibility
under the code.
Assuming that you resolve the situation, your first duty is towards the
contractor. That is not to say that you can condone shoddy workmanship
or materials which are less in quality than what is specified, but you will
be just as interested in checking that the contractor's operatives do not
produce work of a significantly higher standard than specified. You must
exercise your skills competently.
If you work in an ordinary contract management capacity for the contractor, you must expect that independent architects will impute to you whatever motives they would normally impute to the contractor himself. In
particular they will probably assume that your only pre-occupation is the
profit element of the contract. This will be hard to bear since you will,
quite rightly, consider yourself imbued with the highest professional
standards. The only answer is to show them that you are in tune with their
thinking. It can best be done when you are discussing an actual problem
on site. The truth is that the nature of your work will bring you in close
contact with the difficulties of work on site and you will have greater sym-
pathy for the operatives than would an independent architect.

Fig 4.19

Setting out your position to the contractor's client

Dear Sir

[*Heading*]

I refer to your telephone call this morning and I confirm that I will call at your office to discuss your requirements on [*insert date*] at [*insert time*].

This is probably a good opportunity to point out that, as architect to this company, I will be providing you with the normal architectural service. However, since I am employed by a contractor who will carry out the work on site, you may feel that you wish to obtain your own independent architectural advice with regard to quality or budgetary control now or at some later stage. That is your right if you wish to do so and you can be assured that it will not affect my own position.

Yours faithfully

Staff Architect [*or whatever title is appropriate*]

Fig 4.20

If the architect has made an error on his drawing and refuses to take your advice

Dear Sir

[*Heading*]

I refer to our discussion this morning when I made some suggestions which I consider would improve the details shown on your drawing number [*insert number*].

I know that you did not agree with me and I have given the matter further thought. It appears to me that my earlier suggestions were, in fact, valid. Indeed, if we attempt to proceed as shown on your drawing, the result may well be far more expensive than necessary.

With the thought that, perhaps, I did not express myself as clearly as I could have done this morning, I have made a rough sketch, which I enclose, showing what I propose. When you have had time to examine it alongside your own drawing, please let me have your comments.

Yours faithfully

As an architect within the contractor's organisation, you are actually in an excellent position to make helpful suggestions to independent architects with whom you may work. If you can convince them that you are really trying to be helpful, the relationship can be fruitful for all concerned. Be careful, the architectural ego can be a fragile thing.

If the project architect is younger and less experienced than you, he may be on his guard against what he sees as the contractor's attempts to make him look foolish. In such a case, be prepared to go to some trouble to avoid causing him embarrassment back at his own office. In general, if you think he has made a mistake, get into the habit of putting the point to him over the telephone or, better still, meeting him on site. If you can secure his trust, you will have made a useful contribution to the efficient progress of the work. Remember that your ability to liase successfully with other architects is probably one of the main reasons why the contractor employs you. Do not, of course, compromise the contractor's interests. If the architect does not respond to your suggestions orally, you must immediately confirm in writing as necessary. If, for example, you have received a drawing from the architect which you consider is not correct and he fails to see your point of view, Fig 4.20 is the kind of letter you might consider sending, depending upon all the circumstances.

In your relations with other parties, local authorities, statutory undertakings, sub-contractors and suppliers, you should have no particular problems related to your employment by a contractor.

4.10 Gifts

The giving and receiving of gifts in business is bad practice. It can also amount to bribery and corruption, which is a criminal offence with severe penalties under the Prevention of Corruption Acts 1889 to 1916. Under many standard form contracts, the employer is entitled to determine the contractor's employment if he indulges in such corrupt practices (e.g., GC/Works/1, clause 55; JCT 80, clause 27.3).

An element of corruption is secrecy. Thus, if the contractor delivers an expensive pice of stereo equipment quietly to your home and you accept it, you are both guilty of corruption. The fact that you have not repaid the favour is of no consequence. The implication is present that you will be likely to favour the contractor in the future.

Occasionally a contractor or supplier may offer your an 'all expenses paid' trip to the other end of the country to see a new development. There may, indeed, be a legitimate advantage to be gained on behalf of the client if you accept. However, you accept at your peril. In such a case the correct procedure is to declare the offer immediately to your client. Let him decide. If he agrees that you should go and, better still, decides to go with you, there is little chance that you could be accused of corruption because everything is out in the open. It must be emphasised, however, that it is not a good policy to accept even in these circumstances and you should point this out to your client (Fig 4.21).

It has long been the custom for contractors and suppliers to give presents to architects at Christmas. The general rule is that all gifts should be returned to the sender with a brief note of appreciation for the thought (Fig 4.22). Each office will have its own policy, but if you wish to acquire a reputation for complete integrity, refuse all gifts in whatever form they take.

There is probably very little chance that you will be corrupted by accepting a diary or calendar or one bottle of wine, but be careful. In particular, do not accept invitations to have lunch with the contractor or suppliers. It may be difficult to refuse if you are at a site meeting and the contractor suddenly produces a tray of drinks and sandwiches. You should have timed the meeting better (see section 4.5.3) but there is probably safety in numbers on this occasion. Avoid those cosy little lunches in which you are on a one to one basis with a supplier. It may be perfectly innocent on your part, but the fact that you have accepted hospitality may influence you in the future when you are considering what product to specify. That, of course, is just what the supplier intends. It is blind to pretend that the supplier is wining and dining you purely out of good nature. There is nothing wrong with having contractors or suppliers as friends, but in such circumstances you must take extra care that your conduct is above reproach.

It is accepted that you will occasionally take the client out to lunch. Your motives are, of course, exactly the same as those of the contractor and supplier; you are hoping for further work. Even here, you must take care. If the client is a large public body, for example a local authority, it is not acceptable that you give any favours to the officers of that authority. Indeed, you will find that they will not accept them. In the case of a small private client, the situation is different and, provided that you direct your lunch invitation to the client himself and not to his agents or employees, there should be no suggestion of corruption.

The golden rule is not to give or receive gifts of any kind. If you must break this rule, give sparingly to your client, not to his employees.

If you need some concrete on your drive, ask a contractor who is not engaged on one of your firm's contracts to do it and pay him in full.

Fig 4.21

Architect to employer if contractor offers a free trip

Dear Sir

[*Heading*]

I have received a letter from the contractor this morning, dated [*insert date*], a copy of which is enclosed.

As you can see, the contractor is offering [*insert the nature of the contractor's offer*]. Since I am acting as your agent, I have a duty to inform you of all matters of this kind.

Although there is no doubt that the visit would be advantageous, [*indicate briefly in what way it would be advantageous*], it is never advisable to accept offers of this kind because it can complicate the administration of the contract at a later date. I am sure that you can see the implications.

Unless I hear from you in the next day or so that you particularly wish to accompany me on this visit, I propose to decline the offer with a brief note of thanks in accordance with my usual practice.

Yours faithfully

Fig 4.22
Returning gift to sender

Dear Sir

Thank you for your gift which I received today.

In returning the gift to you, I am following my
normal policy. I am sure you understand that I can
do nothing which would tend the throw the slightest
doubt upon my professional integrity.

I do, however, appreciate the thought which prompted
your action.

Yours faithfully

4.11 Summary

o   Not only must you be efficient, you must be seen to be efficient.
o   Unless you have a personal telephone, sit as far away from the office telephone as possible.
o   Cultivate the telephonist.
o   Return telephone calls promptly.
o   Always take notes of telephone calls.
o   Deal with all telephone calls at two periods during the day.
o   Make notes before you write a letter.
o   Write your letters as though they will be read out in court one day.
o   Beware of acknowledging letters.
o   Few people can dictate well.
o   Sign your own name 'on behalf of' the firm.
o   Never use compliments slips.
o   Write a report rather than a long complicated letter.
o   Write a short letter rather than a report.
o   Do not convene unnecessary meetings.
o   In terms of participants at meetings, fewer achieve more.
o   Thoroughly prepare for every meeting.
o   Make the agenda suit the meeting, not the other way around.
o   Avoid working lunches.
o   Make sure that you write the minutes.
o   Never 'fiddle' your time-sheet.
o   Thoroughly understand your filing system and keep your own files in order.
o   Cultivate the print man.
o   Know the limitations of the print machine.
o   If you are working for a contractor, your value lies in the fact that you are an architect.
o   Never accept gifts.

Specific architectural skills

5.1 Surveys

5.1.1 General

Under the general title of 'survey', you may be involved in carrying out inspections and preparing reports or doing a very detailed measured survey and preparation of measured drawings. Your client may be vague about what is required, so get it straight at the beginning and save yourself abortive work. Of course, in many instances, the survey will be necessitated as a result of a brief from your client to carry out new building work in which case, you will be advising the client regarding his particular needs.

Strictly, 'survey' refers to measuring. If you are commissioned to design a building, it may be a new building on a virgin site, the alteration of an existing building or any combination of the two. If the site is relatively large and the building entirely new, it may be worth while advising your client to engage the services of a surveyor to carry out the work. In general, however, it makes more sense to carry out the survey yourself. In doing the work, you will become knowledgeable about the site in a way which is quite impossible by simply studying the survey drawing or even walking around the site with it. A list of basic equipment is given in Fig 5.1.

Most surveys involve some building survey because it is now relatively rare to deal with a totally virgin site. In such circumstances, you must do the survey yourself. Even the very best and most carefully drawn out survey prepared by a surveyor will not contain the information you will be able to commit to paper (and to memory).

Before you actually arrive on site to do the work, check the following points:

o   The address. Many architects have set off to do a survey only to find themselves in the embarrassing position of having to telephone the office to discover where they are supposed to be going. This does nothing for your efficiency image. It has also been known for an architect to measure the wrong site or building.

o   The keys or other means of access. Arrangements for entry are often complex. If the client gives you keys, make sure that they are all there.

o   Boundaries. It is not your job to verify boundaries. Make sure that you obtain a drawing from your client showing their position and extent. Very often, this drawing will be the deed plan, but take care because deed plans are notorious for their vagueness. If you have the slightest doubt, ask your client to arrange for his solicitor to clarify the boundaries for you.

o   Existing plans. Existing plans of a building can be extremely useful in pointing up relationships of parts of the building which you might not suspect, but do not put any trust in them and check everything. Old site plans often show ancient underground features or the presence of previous buildings on what appears to be a clear site.

o   Equipment. See list in Fig 5.1.

Fig 5.1
Basic surveying equipment

o   Steel tapes
o   Folding measuring laths
o   Ranging rods
o   Wooden pegs and lump hammer
o   Yellow wax crayon
o   Dumpy level and staff
o   Binoculars
o   Spirit-level
o   Plumb-bob
o   Camera
o   Torch
o   Mirror
o   Probe
o   Manhole keys
o   Pick
o   Drain stain
o   Survey board
o   Coloured pencils

5.1.2 Procedure

If you are to erect a new building on the site or carry out alteration works to an existing building, you will find that it is better to do the measuring first and prepare the drawings before you take any notes. This is because, during the measuring process, you will always discover important items which could be overlooked in a purely visual inspection.

Always have a quick walk around the site or, if it is a building, a quick look into every room before you begin the survey. You will need to do this in any case so that you can do sketches on which to put your measurements, but if you do not make yourself look into every corner, you may be tempted to assume more than you should.

The measured survey itself should be a straightforward exercise which should cause no problems. The inspection of property or site deserves a few words if only because it is, for some unaccountable reason, a rather neglected part of architectural education. In taking the measurements, you will have been able to get the 'feel' of the property or site. This is important in preparing you for what to expect when you begin to note things in detail. Unless you have been asked to prepare a special report on the property, you will find it easiest to note down the condition on a room by room basis or, if you are dealing with a site, by taking the site in sections.

It is customary to inspect buildings by starting on the top floor and working down. Roof spaces and cellars are normally left to the end to avoid spreading dirt around the interior. Inspect each room from left to right, leaving the corridor or landing until the end. Inspect the exterior of a building elevation by elevation. You must always traverse the boundaries of the site when doing your inspection, no matter how difficult, or uncomfortable, it may be. The ideal is to walk over every part of the site.

If you require any site investigation procedures it is usually best to arrange for them to take place during the time you are carrying out your survey. In this way, you will be able to see what is happening and you will be on hand (but not just standing about) to answer any queries and make any decisions necessary. Other items you should note at the same time are:

o   Position of services, together with depths, etc.
o   Soil tests.
o   Planning and highway aspects.
o   Neighbouring property.
o   Easements.
o   Access.

5.2   Design

5.2.1   The brief

The process of drawing up a good brief involves listening to what the client thinks he wants and writing it down in the form of what the client actually needs. In many cases, your client will present you with a list of what he wants included in the building or even a drawing of the building itself as he envisages it. The client often totally misunderstands your role. He possibly considers that you are simply there to make it technically possible for his own design to be constructed. Commercial clients, in particular seem to be attracted to the notion of producing little sketches, while large organisations with their own estates departments will often present very detailed briefing notes.

Sketches can be very useful in getting into the client's mind, but the danger of very detailed instructions from the client is that it is tempting to regard them as the brief. Whatever you receive from the client only becomes the brief after you have analysed it thoroughly and amended it in the light of your experience, your research into the building type, and research into the habits of your client.

In a great many cases, the brief is the result of sitting down and talking to the client who may well have little idea of what he wants. This situation is potentially the most fruitful, because the client has no preconceived ideas and the brief will gradually emerge under your guidance. There are published guidelines for the production of briefs and, in the case of large developments, you will certainly be well advised to develop your brief by the use of formal techniques. However, in all but the smallest commissions, the general process of briefing should follow the following pattern or something very like it:

o   Meet the client for a general chat about the project.
o   Inspect his existing premises, if relevant.
o   Obtain brief in reasonable amount of detail.
o   Carry out research into building type
                      client's business, habits, etc.
o   Meet client for final tidying up of queries related to the brief.

Above all, you must resist the temptation to start designing the building before you have clarified the whole of the brief. The design must flow naturally from the detailed analysis of your client's needs.

5.2.2   Designing

There are numerous theories of design. Every architect has his own and you are entitled to have yours, but do not inflict it upon your client. He will be unlikely to understand. In other words, you should obviously design the building in the way which you consider is best, but do not make the mistake of thinking that you can convince your client of the worth of your design by trying to explain to him some of the more abstruse aspects of design theory. In ninety-nine cases out of a hundred, your client is simply interested in the basics, i.e., will it keep out the rain? Will it be warm enough? Will it function well overall? etc. Provided that you cater (as you should) for all these points, your client should be satisfied.

The RIBA Plan of Work assumes that you will approach your design in three easy stages: Outline Proposals, Scheme Design and Detail Design. The first stage in which you set out a broad approach to the problems, the second stage in which you firm up your design and the final stage, merging with the start of working drawings, in which you complete the design of every last detail of your scheme. That is logical and fits in with most medium-sized jobs. The RIBA Plan of Work is not intended to be a straitjacket, of course, and you should adjust the sequence in order to suit your particular project.

Obviously, you will produce several embryonic schemes before you eventually produce one which satisfies you. It may be that you finish with two schemes which answer the problems in different ways, but each adequately. On no account should you present both schemes to your client. He will find it difficult enough to understand and discuss one scheme. If you present two, he will find it far more than doubly difficult. It is your job to present the best possible scheme to your client. One which you can advise him to accept. Any differences in schemes should be a matter of detail at this stage. Detail which you should have resolved yourself before showing the client your proposals. The correct point at which to resolve the kind of major decisions which could give rise to totally different schemes is at feasibility, when you are justified, indeed you are required, to present the principal options to the client for decision. But at that early stage, you will be directing his attention to a straight choice of options with clearly defined consequences.

If you present your client with two totally different schemes after feasibility stage, it means that you have not put all the important options before your client at the right time.

When you present your design to your client, you should present a report with it (see section 4.4.2.) By all means make an oral presentation at the same time, but a written report enables your client to study what you have to say at leisure. It may not be necessary to include a report with each successive stage of the design, only you can decide that, but if you are dealing with a large scheme, a formal report at each stage may be advisable, if only to keep a record of the progress of the design.

5.2.3. Presentation

The way in which you present the scheme to your client is largely a matter of your personal choice and your talents in presenting a scheme so that the client can understand it. Never overestimate the client's capabilities in this direction. Many, otherwise highly intelligent, businessmen find great difficulty in understanding plans, sections and elevations and yet architects continue to insist on making those plans, sections and elevations the basis of their presentation.

Consider making your presentation around a model of the proposal. This is not a new idea, of course, but the production of a model tends to be restricted to very large schemes or is postponed until the scheme has been accepted when its primary function is to sit on a boardroom table to impress visitors. Get into the habit of producing working models. That is to say, models which clearly explain the scheme at the stage you are at. The model need not be elaborate. Use it to supplement plans and perspectives. When making a presentation, let the client get the idea of the scheme from the model, then elaborate on it by using plans. Indicate what it would actually look like by quickly drawn perspectives. Do not take sections and elevations to show the client. A building never looks like its elevations, and sections are only useful if the levels are exceedingly complicated. Even then a model can explain levels far better.

Plans should be clearly drawn in black and white with room names printed clearly in each room. Do not use a key at the side and number the rooms, the client will find this infuriating. State the scale and include a drawn scale, but do put a few dimensions on the drawing so that the client will get the overall impression you want. If he is very concerned about some particular aspect of the building, the reception area in a hotel, for example, do a separate drawing showing this to a larger scale with an indication of furnishings and finishes on it. Some architects try to blind their clients with virtuoso renderings and intricate drawings. It is a bad policy. If the client does not properly understand your drawing, he may agree to something he does not really want. He will realise his mistake later when the building is in course of erection, or even completed, and nothing can be done about it. It is in your own best interests that the client thoroughly understands and approves. If there is anything which you feel unhappy about, explain it to him and take him with you in the decision to proceed or attempt a revision.

At every stage in the design, get your client's approval to proceed to the next stage (this is where the reports are so useful).

5.3 Consultants

5.3.1 Types

A consultant is anyone you consider necessary to assist in the design and development of your scheme. Common types of consultant are:
o   Quantity surveyor.
o   Structural engineer.
o   Electrical engineer.
o   Mechanical services engineer.
o   Landscape architect.
On small projects, you may feel capable of carrying out the whole of the work yourself. On larger projects, however, your duty is clear. You must recommend to the client that consultants be appointed to deal with the specialised portions of the work which are beyond your own capabilities. Consultants are employed in one of two different ways:
o   Direct appointment by the client. The advantage is that the consultant is directly responsible to the client. Therefore, if he is negligent, the client can take legal action against him directly. If you are using *Architect's Appointment*, clause 3.8 states that the client will hold each consultant, not the architect, directly responsible for competence, general inspection and performance of work entrusted to him. This is a valuable safeguard for your employer which has been upheld in the courts.
o   Direct appointment by you. Although clause 3.8 of *Architect's Appointment* is stated to apply even when the architect appoints the consultant, in practice the client cannot recover from the consultant in contract because he has no contract with him. Therefore, despite what clause 3.8 states, he is likely to take any action in respect of the consultant's negligence against your employer and it will be up to your employer to join the consultant as a third party. For this reason, you must make sure that your employer has an indemnity from the consultant and that the consultant has the appropriate amount of professional indemnity insurance cover to back it up. Also remember to get the client's agreement to additional fees in respect of consultant's services.

5.3.2 Involvement

All consultants should be employed at the first possible moment. In practice, this cannot be until you have clarified the brief with the client. You may have difficulty in persuading him that consultants are necessary, either at all or at the stage you wish them to be engaged. You must be prepared to stand your ground on this one. The client will not thank you later if you have to redesign large portions of the project simply because the consultants' advice was not available (Fig 5.2).

Fig 5.2

Letter from architect to client if client queries early
appointment of consultants

Dear Sir

[*Heading*]

Thank you for your letter of the [*insert date*] and I
note that you decline to appoint consultants for the
above project at this stage.

The erection of a modern building is a very complex
matter. At one time, it was quite possible, indeed
normal, for an architect to deal with every aspect
of a large contract without assistance from anyone
other than his own office staff. Those days are
long gone. With advances in technology, materials
and building science, an architect will advise the
employment of a consultant just as a doctor will
advise referal to a specialist or the solicitor will
obtain counsel's opinion, because a particular field
has become very specialised. When I advised the
appointment of consultants, I was not suggesting a
possiblility, I was indicating a necessity.

Appointment at this stage will be most economical in
the long term. If you delay in appointment, there
may be a considerable amount of abortive work and,
since your delay would be against my direct advice,
such abortive work would become chargeable as extra
fees. I trust that I have put the matter fairly and
plainly and I should be grateful to hear from you on
this subject before my work progresses too far, say
in a week.

Yours faithfully

Whether the appointment is made through your office or directly by the client, you should make sure that the consultant is aware of the extent of the service which will be required from him. Confirm all the details to him at the time of appointment and get his acceptance. By doing so, you will emphasise that he has to shoulder some responsibility.

Make quite clear that all consultants must report to you. Although it is essential that they inspect their own work in progress on site, make clear to them and to the contractor that all instructions will come from you in accordance with the contract. If the consultant wishes to issue an instruction, he must send it to you so that you can issue it as your instruction (if you agree with it). The contractor must be forewarned about visits from the consultant. In theory, the contractor can refuse entry to the site to all except those persons specifically mentioned in the contract. Most standard forms of contract make no mention of consultants. If the contractor decides to be unreasonable about it, you can easily overcome the difficulty by making the consultant your authorised representative for the sole purpose of inspecting his particular part of the work.

Quantity surveyors are usually considered apart from other consultants, probably because the quantity surveyor is noted in most standard form contracts. He is, however, a consultant and he should be appointed and directed in the same way as other consultants subject only to the provisions of the particular contract conditions.

Always ensure that you receive a certificate of practical completion from each consultant (except the quantity surveyor) for his part of the work before you issue your own certificate. In fact, it is a good idea to arrange your own and the consultants' inspections to coincide.

5.4   Production information

5.4.1 Programming work

It is very difficult to programme the preparation of production information for the simple reason that every project differs in many ways. The best that you can do is to base your programme upon previous jobs and a knowledge of how much time you can afford on the basis of your fees.

5.4.2 Drawings, details and schedules

Your design presentation drawings will normally form the starting-point for producing production information. Most architects find that they prefer to do all the details first in draft, followed by smaller scale sections, etc. The schedules are usually left until everything else is nearing completion.

You will have your own ideas about the way in which the information is presented. Always remember that the drawings are not an end in themselves. Since they are a means to an end, it is important that they are the best means available of achieving that end. Do not overlook the possibility of producing a model of really involved parts of the construction for the contractor's benefit.

Whether you think along traditional lines or you intend to produce a set of elemental drawings, be sure that there is one key drawing on which you can note all the detail drawing numbers. Architects still tend to dump vast piles of drawings on the contractor, leaving him to waste hours trying to tie all the details together. Do not try to be smart or follow whatever trend is in vogue, but do try to make life simple for the person-in-charge. If he readily understands your drawings, he will be able to spot errors *before* he builds them.

A word about drawings: the traditional drawing included everything on the one sheet of paper provided it had some relevance to the subject of that particular drawing. Such drawings are apt to be rather complicated, but they have the merit of gathering all appropriate information together. An operative carrying out one part of the work can see why he is doing what he is doing and the consequences if he makes an error. Elemental drawings work, partly at any rate, on the principle that, for example, the bricklayer will be able to carry out his work more efficiently if the drawing contains nothing but brickwork. The idea is quite reasonable except for two things:

o   An operative who does not really know how his contribution assists the final product will have little job satisfaction or pride in his work.

o   The system assumes perfect drawings. The chances of errors being discovered by the site operative, or even the person-in-charge, are slim because an extensive comparison of drawings would be necessary to reveal inconsistencies.

It is possible to schedule almost everything. The discipline of producing schedules will make you aware of aspects of the building which you could otherwise ignore. It will •also make you popular with the quantity surveyor, whose job will be so much easier. Apart from the obvious things such as ironmongery, windows and doors, try scheduling skirtings, architraves, door casings, pipework and connections, etc.

5.5   Tendering

5.5.1 Inviting tenders

You are strongly advised to carry out your tendering procedures strictly in accordance with the *Code of Procedure for Single Stage Selective Tendering 1977* or the *Code of Procedure for Two Stage Selective Tendering.*

When you submit a list of contractors to the client for approval, you must be sure that all the firms are capable of carrying out the work proposed, in terms of size and quality and financial stability.

There are a number of ways in which firms can be included on the tender list:

o   They have done previous work for you and you are satisfied.

o   They have done previous work for the client and he is satisfied.

o   They have written in, asking to be included on the list.

The firms which you will consider for the list will, therefore, fall into two groups:

o   Firms of which you have had experience.

o   Firms of which you have had no experience.

Before including an unknown firm on the list, you should invite them to answer a brief questionnaire (Fig 5.3). One of the questions should relate to referees and you should send another questionnaire to them (Fig 5.4). This holds good even if the firm is suggested by the client. Since you are responsible for advising the client, you must first of all satisfy yourself. It often happens that the client wishes you to include firms because he has some particular business connection with them. In the case of a bank, for example, all contractors and nominated sub-contractors may be drawn from among the bank's customers. The suggestions may not be very sensible, so you must insist on the vetting procedure.

Before sending out the tender documents, you should make sure that all the contractors on your list are able and willing to tender. Get their agreement in writing by sending them a standard letter (Fig 5.5). The letter cannot, of course be binding, but committing themselves to writing will force the contractors concerned to give the matter proper consideration. Always have a 'standby' list of two or three contractors because, no matter how hard you try to ensure that all the contractors will tender, there may be some who change their minds when they receive the actual documents. If you receive queries from contractors during the tender period, copy the questions and your answers to every contractor. It is usually convenient to do this about half way through the tender period, but if the matter is important, you must circulate the information without delay. On no account must the client have any contact with any of the tenderers during this period.

5.5.2   Receiving tenders

Every tenderer must know the time and date which represents the last occasion on which tenders will be received. Tenders received after this time must be returned unopened. There must be no half measures or

Fig 5.3

Questionnaire to prospective tenderers

1. What is the share capital of the firm?

2. Names and addresses of all directors?

3. Address of registered office?

4. Address of main place of business and, if different, address of office from which you intend to control this project?

5. What was the annual turnover of the firm during the last three years?

6. Number and positions of all office-based staff?

7. Number of site operatives permanently employed in each trade?

8. Number of trained supervisory staff permanently on site?

9. Number and value of current contracts on site?

10. Address, date of completion and value of three projects of similar character to that for which tenders are to be invited carried out by your firm during the last five years?

11. Names and addresses of three persons (preferably architects) to whom reference may be made?

Fig 5.4

Questionnaire to contractor's referees

```
Confidential


Contractor:

Proposed value of contract: £

Proposed date for commencement:

Proposed date for completion:

Type of project (residential, office, etc.):


1.  Would you use this firm again?

2.  Was site supervision good, average or poor?

3.  Was head office back-up good, average or poor?

4.  How would you describe the quality of
    workmanship relative to the quality specified?

5.  Was liaison good between head office and site?

6.  Were the contractor's staff helpful and
    efficient?

7.  Would you describe the contractor as looking for
    opportunities to lodge financial claims, as
    opposed to being aware of his reasonable rights?

8.  Did the contractor have good relations with
    sub-contractors, nominated sub-contractors and
    suppliers?

9.  What was the contractor's attitude to employer's
    licensees?

10. Does this firm, in your experience, normally
    complete within the contract period (or extended
    period)?

11. Would you describe this firm as totally
    straightforward and honest?

12. Have you any further comments which might have a
    bearing on whether this firm is included in the
    tender list?
```

Fig 5.5

Letter from architect to contractor, enquiring if the contractor is willing to submit a tender

Dear Sir

[*Heading*]

I have been instructed by my client, [*insert name of client*], to prepare a list of firms willing to tender for the above project. Please inform me in writing, not later than [*insert date*], if you wish to be included. If you are unable to tender on this occasion, it will not prejudice your inclusion on tender lists for other projects under my direction, but you should note that your agreement to tender does not guarantee that you will receive an invitation to do so.

The tendering procedure will be in accordance with the <u>Code of Procedure for Single Stage Selective Tendering 1977</u> and all firms wishing to be included in the tender list will be deemed to have fully informed themselves of its contents. The following is set out for your information:

o Project title:

o Name of employer:

o Name of architect:

o Name of quantity surveyor:

o Names of consultants:

o Site address:

o General description of the work:

o Approximate cost range: £   to £

o Items for which it is anticipated that nominated sub-contractors will be used:

o Form of contract to be used:

Fig 5.5 – *contd.*

o Principal deletions in the contract:

o Special additional clauses:

o Examination and correction of priced bills -
Alternative 1/Alternative 2 [*delete as appropriate*].

o The contract is to be under seal/hand [*delete as appropriate*].

o Anticipated date for possession:

o Period for completion of the works:

o Approximate date for dispatch of tender documents:

o Tender period:

o Tender to remain open for acceptance for [*insert figure*] weeks.

o Liquidated damages:

o Bond required:

Yours faithfully

compromises about this. It is not unknown for tenderers to exchange prices no more than an hour after the appointed time, therefore, a tender which is an hour late has an unfair advantage. You should arrange to open tenders in the presence of the client as soon as possible after tenders are received. If the client gives you express permission, you may open the tenders before seeing the client. In such circumstances, it is a good idea to have the quantity surveyor with you to comment on the prices and witness that the figures you note down on the summary for the client are accurate. The *Code of Procedure* gives very detailed guidance in the event of mistakes being discovered or tenders being qualified. Follow it carefully. Your client may often ask you to ignore the qualification, especially if the tender is low, or examine a late tender. From his point of view, it is all good business practice, getting the best possible deal. You must resist your client's pressure because:

o   The tenderers have each expended large amounts of time and money in preparing their tenders and they have the right to expect that you and the client will stick to the rules which you all understand. It is considered that, depending on the circumstances, tenderers who are aggrieved by the client's conduct in considering tenders might have a cause of action if the client's action contravenes the *Code of Procedure* which has been specifically stated to apply. This consideration should carry great weight with the client.

o   A tenderer who qualifies is seeking what amounts to an unfair advantage. If all tenderers were allowed to qualify as they saw fit, any reasonable yardstick for comparing tenders would be lost.

o   A fair system of tendering benefits the whole industry.

The accepted tender is usually the lowest. Assuming that the bills of quantities have been checked and found accurate or the appropriate procedure has been carried out, the client, or you on the client's behalf, should accept the tender without delay. It should be noted that, under English law, but not under Scottish law, a tender can be withdrawn at any time before acceptance.

5.6   Contracts

It is part of your professional duty to advise the client on the best form of contract for any particular purpose. Many architects use one form for all purposes. If the client suffers loss wholly or partly due to the use of a form which is inappropriate or one which should have been amended, the client may argue that it amounts to professional negligence. You must, therefore, ensure that you are fully informed about the main points of each contract (Fig 5.6). This is an area neglected by large numbers of architects. It

Fig 5.6
Contract selection

Criteria	JCT80 With Quantities	JCT80 Without Quantities	JCT80 With Approximate Quantities	JCT80 With Contractor's Design	IFC84 Intermediate Form	MW80 Minor Works Form	JCT Fixed Fee Form	ACA2	GC/Works/1
Negotiated	○	○	○	○	○	○	○		
Simple						○	◐		
Comprehensive	○	○	○					○	○
Flexible					○	○		○	
Lump sum	○	○		○	○	○		○	○
Bills of quantities can be used	○	◐		○				○	○
Schedule of rates can be used					○	○		○	○
Specification can be used				○		○	○	○	○
Alternative clauses								○	
Suitable for uncertain work							○		
Suitable for complex work	○		○	○				○	○
Suitable for early start work				○			○		
Suitable for contracts over one year	○	○	○	○			○	○	○
Suitable for project management contracts				○				○	
Suitable for contracts under £100,000	○	○	○	○	○	○	○	○	○
Suitable for contracts £100,000 to £800,000	○		○	○	◐		○	○	○
Suitable for contracts over £1,000,000	○		○	○			○	○	○
Principal Topics Covered									
Architect	○	○	○		○	○	○	○	○
Quantity surveyor	○	○	○		○	○	○	○	○
Clerk of works	○	○	○		○		○		○
Contractor's obligations	○	○	○	○	○	○	○	○	○
Discrepancies	○	○	○	○	○	○		○	○
Statutory requirements	○	○	○	○	○	○	○		
Drawings	○	○	○	○	○	○	○	○	○
Ground conditions								○	○

Fig 5.6 – *contd.*

Principal Topics Covered *contd.*

	JCT80 With Quantities	JCT80 Without Quantities	JCT80 With Approximate Quantities	JCT80 With Contractor's Design	IFC84 Intermediate Form	MW80 Minor Works Form	JCT Fixed Fee Form	ACA2	GC/Works/1
Access by architect	O	O	O	O		O	O	O	O
Contractor's supervision of the works	O	O	O	O	O	O	O	O	
Vesting of property	O	O	O	O	O		O	O	O
Insurance against injury to persons and property	O	O	O	O	O	O	O	O	
Insurance of the works	O	O	O	O	O	O	O	O	
Insurance against non-negligent damage to the works	O	O	O	O	O		O	O	
Design indemnity insurance by contractor								O	
Disturbance to regular progress	O	O	O	O	O		O	O	O
Instructions	O	O	O	O	O	O	O	O	O
Valuation of variations	O	O	O	O	O	O		O	O
Assignment	O	O	O	O	O	O	O	O	O
Sub-letting	O	O	O	O	O	O	O	O	O
Named sub-contractors					O			O	
Nominated sub-contractors	O	O	O				O		O
Employer's licensees	O	O	O	O	O		O	O	O
Liquidated damages	O	O	O	O	O	O	O	O	O
Extension of time	O	O	O	O	O	O	O	O	O
Extension of time review	O	O	O	O	O			O	
Acceleration								O	
Postponement	O	O	O	O	O		O	O	O
Deferment of possession					O				
Practical completion	O	O	O	O	O	O	O	O	O
Defects liability period	O	O	O	O	O	O	O	O	O
Partial possession	O	O	O	O			O	O	O
Certification/payment	O	O	O	O	O	O	O	O	O
Fluctuations	O	O	O	O	O			O	O
Determination by employer	O	O	O	O	O	O	O	O	O
Determination by contractor	O	O	O	O	O	O	O	O	

Fig 5.6 – *contd.*

Principal Topics Covered *contd.*

	JCT80 With Quantities	JCT80 Without Quantities	JCT80 With Approximate Quantities	JCT80 With Contractor's Design	IFC84 Intermediate Form	MW80 Minor Works Form	JCT Fixed Fee Form	ACA2	GC/Works/1
Determination by either party						O		O	
Antiquities	O	O	O	O			O	O	O
Hostilities	O	O	O	O		O			
Adjudication								O	
Arbitration	O	O	O	O	O	O	O	O	O
Litigation								O	

is, therefore, an area in which you have ample opportunity to show your competence. Since few architects are interested in contracts for their own sake you can, relatively easily, make yourself the office expert with the aid of suitable books and articles in the professional press. On no account should you leave the filling in of the contract to the client's own solicitors or to the quantity surveyor.

5.7 Summary

o   Do surveys yourself rather than employ a surveyor, unless they are very complicated.

o   Make the client responsible for checking his own boundaries.

o   Measure first, inspect later.

o   In taking a brief, you must give the client what he needs, not what he wants.

o   Do not start to design until the brief is settled.

o   Show the client a design you believe in, not that plus another one, 'just in case'.

o   Present your design in a way the client will understand.

o   Avoid using a key to room names.

o   Consultants should be appointed and paid directly by the client.

o   Make the consultant take responsibility for his own work and issue you with a certificate of practical completion for his own work.

o   Drawings are only a means to an end.

o   Use a drawing system that will make the contractor's work easy.

o   Get into the habit of producing schedules.

o   Use the tendering *Codes*.

o   The client will hold the architect responsible for unsuitable firms on the tender list, even if he has suggested them – he will be quite correct.

o   Always have 'standby' tenderers.

o   You must be aware of the legal implications of different contract forms.

Work in progress

6.1 Introduction

It is not the intention to set out a detailed guide to running a contract. Many other excellent books cover that general area (see Appendix A). This chapter deals with some important aspects in a selected number of contract situations. Emphasis will continue to be placed on techniques to assist you to succeed where others sometimes fail.

6.2 Clerk of works

The clerk of works is mentioned specifically in JCT 80 (clause 12), IFC 84 (clause 3.10) and GC/Works/1 (clause 16). Of these, the JCT 80 provisions are the longest, but not without fault. ACA 2 and MW 80 forms of contract make no express provision for a clerk of works, but that does not prevent you from making such provision in the specification or bills of quanitities. For brevity's sake, the JCT 80 provisions will be taken as applying in this section. If you are using JCT 63, you are treading very dangerous ground. You should have abandoned this form by now.

The clerk of works is to act solely as an inspector. He cannot issue instructions and, if he issues directions, they are of no immediate effect until you have confirmed them in writing (which you must do within 2 days of the date of the direction). When, and if, you confirm them by an instruction, they are effective only from the date of your instruction. The moral is clear. Do not allow the clerk of works to waste time issuing directions. Anything important enough to warrant a direction should be communicated to you immediately by telephone so that you can issue a proper instruction forthwith.

Fig 6.1

Letter from architect to clerk of works on appointment

Dear Sir

[*Heading*]

My client [*insert name*] has confirmed your
appointment as clerk of works for the above
contract. I should be pleased if you would call at
this office on [*insert date*] at [*insert time*] to be
briefed on the project and to collect your copies of
drawings, specification, bills of quantities, weekly
report forms and daily diary.

It is anticipated that the contractor will commence
work on the [*insert date*] by taking possession of the
site. You are expected to be present on site [*insert
periods during which the clerk of works is expected
to be present*]. According to the contractor's
programme, all site accommodation will be complete by
day [*insert day number*] and I should be glad if you
will check that it is as described in the bills.

Your duties will be as described in the contract
[*clause x*] a copy of which is enclosed for your
attention. In particular, I wish to draw your
attention to the following:

1. You will be expected to inspect all workmanship
    and materials to ensure conformity with the
    contract requirements. Any defects must be
    pointed out to the person-in-charge, to whom you
    should address all comments. If any defects are
    left unremedied for twenty-four hours or if they
    are of a major or fundamental nature, you must
    let me know immediately by telephone. Do not
    issue any written directions to the contractor.

Fig 6.1 – *contd.*

2. Although it is common practice for clerks of works to mark defective work on site, you must not make any such marks or in any way deface materials on site.

3. It is not my policy to issue lists of defects to the contractor before practical completion (commonly known as 'snagging lists'). They may be misinterpreted and give rise to disputes. They should be compiled by the person-in-charge. Please confine your remarks to the contractor to oral comments.

4. The architect is the only person empowered to issue instructions to the contractor.

5. You are not empowered to vary work or materials or design. Refer all queries to me.

6. Complete the weekly report sheets, paying especial attention to [*insert as required*], and send them to me each Monday.

7. Complete the diary as fully as possible.

8. Remember that your weekly reports and diary may be called in evidence in the case of a dispute. Bear this in mind when making entries.

I hope that you can achieve the kind of relationship with the contractor on which the successful completion of the contract depends. Do not hesitate to contact me if you are in any doubt about anything.

Yours faithfully

Fig 6.2

Letter from architect to contractor setting out the limits of the authority of the clerk of works

Dear Sir

[*Heading*]

A clerk of works has been appointed for the above
project. His name is Mr [*insert name*] and he is
well experienced in work of this type. I hope that
you will build up a successful relationship over the
coming months.

The clerk of works will be on site during the
whole/part [*omit as appropriate*] of the week only.
His duties are as laid down in the contract [*clause
x*]. I hope it will be helpful if I emphasise that
he is acting as an inspector of materials and
workmanship; he is not empowered to issue any
instructions. Although I expect that he will be
ready to give his advice, if requested, on any
points which arise during construction, the
responsibility for carrying out the works in
accordance with the contract remains yours. Please
note especially that he is in no way a substitute
for your own person-in-charge on site. The duty of
the clerk of works is to the employer although he is
under my direction.

I have informed him that he must not make any marks
on the works to indicate defective materials; I know
this can be a source of annoyance. No 'snagging
lists' will be issued. This should remove any
misunderstandings regarding the extent of defective
work. Any defective workmanship or materials will
be pointed out to the person-in-charge, noted in the
clerk of works' diary and reported to me.

Fig 6.2 – *contd.*

I trust that it will be unnecessary for me to issue
specific instructions on such matters.

If you are in any doubt regarding the contents of
this letter, please do not hesitate to write or
telephone me for clarification.

Yours faithfully

Copy: Clerk of Works

The position should be made clear to the clerk of works when he takes up his appointment (Fig 6.1). If you are wise, you will also emphasise the limits of the clerk of works' authority in a letter to the contractor (Fig 6.2). Of course, there is nothing to prevent you from agreeing other duties with the clerk of works, such as taking measurements, keeping records, etc., but remember that they form part of the contract between the clerk of works and the employer and they have nothing to do with the contractor. If you wish to give the clerk of works additional authority in some specific area, for example, the checking of daywork sheets, you must spell it out to the contractor very carefully (Fig 6.3). In general, it is not wise to give the clerk of works authority to do other than simply inspect and report back to you. The old adage that no man can serve two masters is sound and the contractor will become understandably annoyed if he receives his instructions from the clerk of works and from you.

The clerk of works may be skilled and wise, a fount of good advice for all concerned in the building process. On the other hand, he may be incompetent or lazy. It is not always easy to discover the truth about a clerk of works who may be less than satisfactory until the work on site has been in progress for some time because, by the very nature of his work, he may not come under your close supervision. If he really is not good enough, you must confer with the partner in charge of the project immediately. The clerk of works is appointed by the client and any negligence on the part of the clerk of works lies at the door of the client and at your door also. It may be better, from the client's point of view, to have no clerk of works than a poor one.

It is very much in your interests to see that the client (the 'employer' in the building contract) employs a clerk of works. Recent case law has settled the point. The clerk of works is liable for his negligence. This means that, provided he is employed and paid by the client, the client will be vicariously liable for his actions. This is the situation even though he is under your direction. If he is negligent in his inspections, it will not relieve you of all responsibility, but it may reduce your, or your firm's, liability for damages. Take care that the clerk of works does not overstep his authority by carrying out what he genuinely believes to be his duty because of traditional practices. Two common examples are:

○   Placing chalk marks on defective work.

○   Issuing 'snagging lists'.

Work incorporated into the works on site becomes the property of the client. If it is defective, your remedy is to instruct the contractor to remove it. After the work has been removed, it is undoubtedly the contractor's property to do with as he wishes. The clerk of works is clearly prohibited from defacing the contractor's property in any way. Thus, if the clerk of works puts any mark on work which he considers to be defective, the client

Fig 6.3

Letter from architect to contractor regarding extension of the authority of the clerk of works

Dear Sir

[*Heading*]

I should be pleased if you would note that the clerk

of works [*insert name*] is my authorised

representative for the purpose of clause [*insert*

clause number] of the Contract and for that purpose

alone.

[*Set out a brief description of the authority of the*

clerk of works under the clause]

This extension of the authority of the clerk of

works will apply until further notice, but note that

his other duties remain unaffected.

Yours faithfully

Copies: Clerk of works

             Quantity surveyor

may be liable for the damage. When inspecting the work, the clerk of works should simply make his own notes, point out unsatisfactory work to the person-in-charge and notify you.

It has become traditional for the clerk of works to issue what are known as 'snagging lists'. If the clerk of works does prepare such a list, it has no contractual significance. It binds neither you nor the contractor. The contractor may welcome the list as an indication of what defects remain to be corrected, but there is a danger that he will consider that, when he has attended to all the items on the list, he has fulfilled his obligations. His obligations, of course, are laid down in the contract documents and any instructions you may issue. 'Snagging lists' tend to cause more problems than they solve and they are best avoided. If you tolerate them, never refer to them in your letters. If the contractor mentions them, perhaps in a letter asking you to issue your certificate of practical completion, make the position clear in your reply (Fig 6.4).

6.3   Inspection v supervision

There appears to be a great deal of confusion between inspection and supervision in the minds of clients, contractors and even judges – who might be expected to have the distinction especially clear. Much of the confusion is certainly due to the fact that architects often refer to supervision when they really mean inspection. The JCT forms of contract, with their alternative 'Supervising Officer', have not helped matters since 'Supervising Officer' is always associated in the contract with 'Achitect'. IFC 84 has attempted to clarify the situation by inserting 'the' before 'Supervising Officer', but it is doubtful whether it will be effective. It might be prudent to cross out the words 'Supervising Officer' wherever they appear in the contract so that no one is given the wrong impression. The RIBA *Architect's Appointment* states quite clearly, in clause 3.10;

'The architect will visit the site at intervals appropriate to the stage of construction to inspect the progress and quality of the works and to determine that they are being executed generally in accordance with the contract documents. The architect will not be required to make frequent or constant inspections.'

The architect's services are stated, in clause 1.22, as being:

'Visit the site as appropriate to inspect generally the progress and quality of the work.'

Inspection involves looking and noting and possibly carrying out tests. Supervision, on the other hand covers inspection, but also the issuing of directions of a detailed nature regarding the carrying out of the works. Supervision is the responsibility of the contractor. Inspection is the responsibility of the architect and the clerk of works.

Fig 6.4

Letter from architect to contractor if 'snagging lists' mentioned

Dear Sir

[*Heading*]

Thank you for your letter of the [*insert date*]. I
will inspect the works and issue my certificate of
practical completion if I am satisfied that
practical completion has been achieved.

I note your reference to 'snagging lists'. You are,
of course, aware that the contract does not
recognise any such lists. Although I have no
particular objection if the clerk of works goes
beyond his specific duties and gives you an
indication of defective work in written form, it
must be clear that he is not producing a definitive
list of defective work, but simply trying to assist
the person-in-charge. The carrying out of the works
in accordance with the contract will always remain
your responsibility alone.

Yours faithfully

Copy: Clerk of works

Fig 6.5

Letter from architect to client if client complains about the architect's 'supervision' of the job

Dear Sir

[*Heading*]

Thank you for your letter of the [*insert date*].

I share your concern about the standard of supervision on this project and I enclose a copy of a letter which I have written to the contractor on this topic. If there is no improvement over the course of the next week I intend to have a meeting with the managing director of [*insert name of the contractor*] and make the point in clear terms.

I think it is probable that you have not fully understood the nature of my own duties in this regard. My duty is to <u>inspect</u> the work so that I can take appropriate action if the work is not progressing properly in accordance with the contract. <u>Supervision</u> is solely the duty of the contractor. It implies a degree of direction which only he can give since the works are under his control. It is clear that the contractor is performing his duty to supervise in a less than satisfactory manner as my own inspections reveal. I am taking what action is open to me under the contract. If I consider it necessary that drastic action be taken, I will write to you again.

Yours faithfully

Never refer to your 'supervision' of the site, either in a letter or orally, or you may be taken to assume more responsibility than you have. There is no way that you can properly supervise building work unless you insert a clause in the contract to the effect. By doing so, you would effectively move the responsibility for the proper and timely completion of the works from the contractor to yourself; not something you would wish to do. If, as sometimes happens, you receive a letter from the client complaining that he is not happy with your 'supervision' of the job, you should make sure that he understands the position (Fig 6.5).

There are some excellent books on the subject of inspection (Appendix A) and it is not proposed to repeat all the good advice here. However, there are a few points which should be borne in mind when you are entrusted with the administration of a contract:

o   If possible, time your inspections to coincide with particularly important operations on site. Too many architects treat site inspections as something to be done in between other jobs and preferably on a fine day. An inspection carried out on a dull and rainy day may surprise the contractor and tell you a lot about the way he is running the project.

o   Know what you are going to inspect before you set out. If you simply arrive on site and wander aimlessly, looking at the work in a random fashion, you will be playing into the hands of an unscrupulous contractor, who will certainly make sure that skimped work is not immediately obvious.

o   Inspect alone or with the clerk of works. The person-in-charge may offer to accompany you, but his purpose may be to direct your attention away from parts of the building. By inspecting alone, you can follow your prepared schedule. When you have finished what you set out to see, it then does no harm to wander at random if you have time. If you are doubtful about anything you see on site, wait until you have completed your inspection and then take the person-in-charge to see the item in question.

o   When you return to the office, take any action necessary following your inspection (such as issuing an instruction to remove defective work) then file your inspection notes. These notes could be important, particularly if any question of latent v patent defects arises after the issue of the final certificate.

o   If the contractor asks you to make a decision when you visit the site, if possible wait until you are back in the office before giving your decision in writing. Few things are so urgent that an immediate decision is required. A decision given on site is made under pressure from the contractor. Unless the subject matter is very minor, you will decide to amend the decision later, when you have had time to give it proper consideration. A decisive man is not the man who gives instant decisions, but the one who knows when instant decisions are unnecessary.

6.4 Architect's instructions

You may only give instructions if the contract expressly empowers you to do so. Even then, your power to issue instructions is limited to those instructions noted in the contract. That means that you cannot simply issue instructions about anything at all. Before you issue any instructions which have implications on the cost of the work or the time period, you must obtain authority from the client. This is also the case if you intend materially to vary the design although there may be no cost implication. It is good practice to issue instructions on a printed form headed 'Architect's Instruction'. The instruction should be clear, stating whether you are adding, omitting varying the work or simply clarifying something. Give amounts involved and also the location. If there is any room for doubt, a location drawing should be included. The instruction should refer to the clause empowering issue and it should be dated and signed by the architect named in the contract. The person signing the instruction must be registered, not simply a technician, no matter how experienced he may be. An example of an instruction is shown in Fig 6.6.

Although the use of printed Architect's Instruction forms is recommended, an instruction is still valid provided that it is issued in writing. Therefore, a letter may be an instruction, depending on its contents. The advantage of using the printed forms is that it simplifies the business of cost control of the contract as work proceeds. Unless you specifically *instruct* the contractor to do something (or in some instances to do nothing), you have not issued an instruction. Thus, if you send a drawing to the contractor, it is not an instruction to do the work shown thereon. It may be simply inviting comment or even an invitiation to him to do the work without payment. If you send the contractor a drawing without any accompanying instruction, you have only yourself to blame if he does nothing. Beware, however, because most contractors would take the issue of a drawing as being an instruction to do the work.

Although all your instructions must be in writing, most forms of contract (but not IFC 84) make provision in case you issue an oral instruction. Unless the contract expressly provides otherwise, oral instructions are of no immediate effect. They only become effective from the date you confirm them in writing. Therefore, there would appear to be little point in issuing instructions orally. In practice, of course, contractors usually do take notice of oral instructions on the assumption that you will confirm them as soon as you can. From the contractor's point of view, he is taking a risk. It is most important, therefore, that you are scrupulous in confirming oral instructions. It is difficult to see the excuse for oral instructions because it is quite simple to carry a duplicate book with you so that you can confirm any urgent instructions on the spot. It is very much in your

Fig 6.6

Architect's instruction

ACA

ARCHITECT'S INSTRUCTION

Architect's name: I. M. Cumming

Address: 9 Anolay Terrace, Sloughly

To –   No. 101

                              Date 14 February 1986

Contractor's name: Gerry Builders Ltd   Job reference IMC/GB/2345

Address: 2 The Shambles

          Fayling Quiklie

Works: Shops and Flats, Alinor Row, Nether Fayling, Herts

Instructions

Clause 8.1(e)

Omit   Bill of quantities item 72F (brass door knockers) 17 no.

                          item 32G (brass letter plates) 17 no.

Add   Anodised aluminium bell push assembly
           obtained from Plain Fixtures Ltd
           cat. no. PF/000012   17 no.

           Anodised aluminium letter plates
           obtained from Fancy Fixtures Ltd
           cat. no. FF/001/345/9   17 no.

Signed _I.M. Cumming_ _____ Architect

✓	Employer	✓ c/w.	☐	☐
✓	Contractor	☐	☐	☐
✓	Architect	☐	☐	☐

© Association of Consultant Architects 1982

interest to do so in order that the contractor has no excuse if he fails to take immediate action on an urgent matter.

If the contractor confirms an instruction to you, it is a sign that you are losing control of the job. The first rule is: do not issue oral instructions. The second rule is: if you must issue an oral instruction, confirm it yourself immediately you return to the office, at the latest, and get it off in that day's post. The danger in the contractor confirming your instruction is that he will confirm it in a way which suits him. That is natural, and it may also serve to inform you that he has not properly understood what you want. The problem is, that by the time you receive his confirmation the work may be done. No matter, you can still refute his confirmation, at least in the terms he has stated, and he is not due for payment, but it sours relations. Most standard forms of contract provide for the situation if the contractor fails to comply with your instruction. Generally, the client is entitled to employ another firm to do the work. Before taking this step, you should send a notice to the contractor requiring compliance within whatever period is stipulated in the contract (Fig 6.7 is a notice to be issued under the JCT 80 form). If the contractor does not comply, it is wise to obtain competitive quotations from three other firms for carrying out the work. Then the contractor will be unable to argue convincingly later that the employer could have had the work done at a cheaper price. The employer is normally entitled to deduct the cost of having the work carried out, including your additional fees, from any money due or to become due to the contractor. It is clearly better if you can persuade the contractor to do the work himself. If you meet this kind of problem, telephone him before you issue the compliance notice and find out why the work is not being done. It may be an oversight on his part. Do not be put off more than a day or two. The trouble most often seems to arise in the case of instructions to remove defective work. The contractor no doubt considers that it is not defective and perhaps thinks that if he bides his time, you will forget or the work will be covered up and you will hesitate to insist on removal, especially if the defect is a matter of quality. Remember the maxim: 'He who hesitates is lost'.

Finally, always issue your instructions in good time. Failure to do so will result in the contractor claiming extensions of time and possibly direct loss and/or expense.

6.5   Cost control

Cost control of a project should begin, obviously, at brief stage. Remember that if you overspend, your employer could forfeit his fees and possibly face a claim for damages from the client. Therefore, make sure that the

Fig 6.7
Letter from architect to contractor, requiring compliance with
instruction [in accordance with JCT 80]

REGISTERED POST OR RECORDED DELIVERY

Dear Sir

[*Heading*]

Take this as notice under clause 4.1.2 of the

Conditions of Contract that I require you to comply

with my instruction number [*insert number*] dated

[*insert date*], a further copy of which is enclosed.

If you have not complied with this notice within

seven days of receipt, the employer may employ and

pay other persons to execute any work whatsoever

which may be necessary to give effect to the

instruction. All costs incurred in connection with

such employment will be deducted from money due or

to become due to you under the contract or will be

recovered from you as a debt.

Yours faithfully

Copies: Client

        Quantity surveyor

initial estimate is realistic. Ideally, you should work closely with the quantity surveyor throughout all the design and development stages so that the lowest tender figure is very near to the original estimate. Nothing will endear you to the client more than producing a finished building which is slightly under the original estimate. During the progress of the job, you should insist that the quantity surveyor gives you monthly updates on the state of finances and a corrected forecast of the final figure. It is good practice to send this breakdown to the client (Fig 6.8).

If the client requires any additions, omissions or alterations in the work, it is essential that you inform him, before you issue your instruction, how much the change will cost. Get his written acceptance of the extra cost or confirm his acceptance to him (Fig 6.9).

Usually, you will require the quantity surveyor to value the work each month before you issue your certificate. It is however, your certificate, not the quantity surveyor's. You will be responsible for over-certification. Remember to inform the quantity surveyor each month of any defects which are not to be valued (Fig 6.10). If you are of the opinion that the quantity surveyor has overvalued any part of the work, you are entitled to, indeed you must, amend the amount on your certificate. None of the standard forms makes any interim certificate conclusive, so if you discover an overvaluation you may correct it on the next certificate.

6.6   Extensions of time

Every standard form of contract has different provisions regarding extensions of time. It is important to keep the particular provisions clearly in mind when the contractor notifies you of any delay. Essentially, extension of time provisions are in the contract to protect the client's right to deduct liquidated damages if the contract overruns the contract completion date. If the overrunning is due to a default of the client or his agents (this means you), the right to deduct liquidated damages will be lost unless an adequate extension is given. You can only give an extension if the contract expressly provides for it. Some contracts provide for the award of extensions of time for delay due to any default of the client (ACA 2 for example); others, like the JCT series, provide for all the more common defaults of the client. The client will also lose his right to deduct liquidated damages if you have not awarded proper extensions of time in respect of any of the other matters which are listed in the contract as grounds for an extension.

The other matters are occurrences which would not, of themselves, give the contractor any right to an extension, unlike client's defaults, but which are included in the list. Such things as *force majeure*, exceptionally adverse weather and shortages of labour or materials may be included.

Fig 6.8
Monthly statement of finance

	ADD	OMIT
Contract sum		
Contingencies		
PC sums		
Provisional sums		
Architect's instructions (to instruction no.)		
Measured work		
Fluctuations		
Contractor's claims for loss and/or expense under clause		
Sundry items (specify)		

Forecast Final Cost   £_____

Fig 6.9

Letter from architect to client, confirming cost of additional work

Dear Sir

[*Heading*]

I refer to your letter of the [*insert date*] and my telephone conversation with you this morning regarding the additional [*insert the nature of the additional work*].

I confirm:

1. The estimated cost of the additional work will be £[*insert sum*]. This sum will be added to the contract sum.

2. You approve this cost and wish me to instruct the contractor to put the work in hand as soon as possible.

Yours faithfully

Copy: Quantity surveyor

Fig 6.10
Letter from architect to quantity surveyor regarding defective
work

Dear Sir

[*Heading*]

The following defective work has been noted on the
above site:

[*insert list of defective work in sufficient detail
to enable the quantity surveyor to identify it -
include items from previous months until the defects
have been corrected*]

The above mentioned work is to be <u>omitted</u> from your
next valuation.

Yours faithfully

The contractor's notice informing you of delay is not usually considered to be a pre-requisite before you can grant an extension of time, but under JCT 80 and IFC 84 terms the contractor must notify all delays, howsoever caused. Most standard forms allow for some sort of review of extensions of time to take place after practical completion in order to protect the client's rights. In practice, this means that, if the contractor gives you no notification during the progress of the work, you are obliged to consider what extensions should be granted as soon as the review period becomes operative. You must then grant extensions for any client defaults. Most standard forms lay down time limits for the grant of extensions. If so, you must scrupulously adhere to them. If there are no time limits, you should issue your grant, or state that no grant is due, within a reasonable time of receiving all particulars, as dictated by the contract, from the contractor. A reasonable time will depend on the nature of the delay. If it is continuing, you can wait until it has finished and then grant the extension or, if that appears to be unduly hard on the contractor, you can issue an interim grant covering delay up to a particular date and consider the remaining delay when it has finished. If the delay has already come to an end, it is probably reasonable to expect you to grant your extension within 12 weeks (the period specified in JCT 80).

In granting your extension, you are expected to give an estimate only. You are not expected to be precise unless the circumstances of the delay are sufficiently clear cut. The estimate must be fair and reasonable after taking all the circumstances into account. What is fair and reasonable depends on your judgment, not on the opinion of the client who must take no part in your deliberations, neither has he any power or veto if he disagrees with your view. It is wise, however, to inform the client regarding any grant so that he is fully in the picture.

Do not give any reasons for your grant. If you do, the contractor will continue the argument.

Many architects seem to misunderstand the meaning of liquidated damanges. They are a genuine pre-estimate of the damages likely to be incurred by the client if the job overruns. They must be estimated as accurately as possible (and that may not be very accurately) at tender stage. They can be deducted by the client, at his sole discretion, without further proof of damage. They may even be deducted if no damage, in the event, has occurred. The contractor often refers to liquidated damages, incorrectly, as penalties. A penalty, which is not enforceable, is a sum of money which bears no possible relation to the injury sustained; it is simply a punishment. There appears to be no reported case on building contracts where a liquidated damages sum has been disallowed on the grounds of its being a penalty.

6.7   Financial claims

Financial claims can take various forms:

o   Contractual claims – these are the only claims which you are empowered to decide.

o   Common law claims – claims which the contractor may make in pursuance of his rights under the general law.

o   *Ex-gratia* claims – claims which have no legal foundation. They are sometimes known as moral or hardship claims.

Few contractors know how to submit a good claim. Many architects spend far too much time trying to sort out claims and doing the contractor's work for him. You have no duty to make a claim for the contractor, nor even to tell him that he should claim in particular circumstances. In fact, your duty to the client almost certainly means that you must not indicate to the contractor when he should claim. Before you consider the contractor's claim, you should be sure that it is submitted entirely and precisely in accordance with the contract provisions. Refuse to consider it until all the conditions have been met. When it seems clear that the contractor has met all the conditions, but his claim is still badly set out, give him an ultimatum – either he properly substantiates every part of his claim or he must take the consequences in the form of receiving less than he expects (Fig 6.11).

If you handle claims in this way, you will save yourself an enormous amount of time. When you actually come to consider a claim, it must be perfectly clear what the contractor is claiming and why. Do not hesitate to reject claims, or any part of them, that are ambiguous. Remember that the odds are stacked against the contractor:

o   The contractor may or may not claim.

o   If he does, he may or may not convince you.

o   If you reject the claim, he may or may not take the matter further.

o   If he takes it further, he has to convince the arbitrator or the judge.

o   If he wins, it may not be worth the trouble.

o   If he loses, he is worse off than before.

The pressure, (see Fig 6.12) therefore, is on the contractor, not on you or on the client. The important thing is to keep calm.

Every building contract has its own provisions for financial claims. You must ensure that they are followed exactly. Most of the troubles in regard to claims stem from the fact that both architect and contractor fail to read the provisions carefully.

If part of the contractor's claim is a common law or *ex-gratia* claim, you must set it aside and refer it to the client for determination. Try to avoid being drawn into the decision-making process on such claims. You have no authority and although the client may well ask for your advice, it

---

Fig 6.11

Letter from architect to contractor if claim not properly presented

Dear Sir

[*Heading*]

I refer to your claim for loss and/or expense under
clause [*insert clause number*] of the Conditions of
Contract.

It appears, at first sight, that you have complied
with all the procedural conditions which you are
obliged to satisfy before I can consider your claim.
However, the claim is very badly set out, difficult
to understand and, in parts, poorly substantiated.
I am quite prepared to examine the claim as it
stands, but I should warn you that it is my duty to
reject any part of it if I am not entirely satisfied
of its validity.

Please consider whether you wish to resubmit your
claim in a more appropriate form. I will postpone
my consideration for seven days to give you an
opportunity to make your decision.

Yours faithfully

Copy: Quantity surveyor

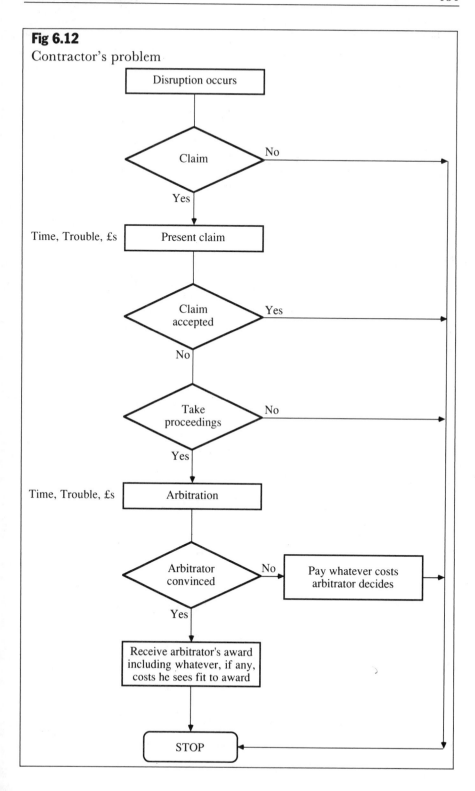

Fig 6.12
Contractor's problem

remains his decision. In contrast, contractual claims are entirely your province and the client has no right to interfere with your decisions. It is always wise, however, to send the client a brief report about the claim and the decision you have reached.

Most forms of contract require you to 'ascertain' claims for loss and/or expense. That means that the amounts must be worked out precisely. That can be contrasted with claims for extension of time, when you are simply required to 'estimate' the amount of time. You would be well advised to leave the ascertaining of amount of financial claim to the quantity surveyor, but you must decide first if the claim is valid. It is your decision, not something which can be delegated to the quantity surveyor.

Deciding whether a claim is valid depends essentially on marshalling the facts and applying logical thought processes to them. This procedure is much simplified if you have required the contractor to supply you with a programme of work based on network analysis or a precedence diagram. Finally, remember that financial claims may have no relationship to claims for extension of time. The contractor may have a perfectly valid claim for loss and/or expense despite finishing the contract on time. On the other hand, he may have a good claim for receiving an extension, but no entitlement for financial recompense. Always consider the claims separately.

6.8   Practical completion

JCT series of contracts refer to 'Practical Completion', other forms use different terminology. Although there is conflicting case law, it can be said that, in general, practical completion may be certified when only very minor defects are apparent. It is something for your opinion. It does not depend upon the contractor's view or upon the view of the client. Very often, the client will be willing to take possession of the works before you are ready to certify that they are practically complete. Some forms of contract expressly provide for that eventuality.

The contractor is not obliged to notify you when he considers that practical completion has been achieved, but normally he will do so. It is not unknown for the contractor to notify practical completion long before it actually occurs. In these circumstances, visit the site as requested, inspect the work and if it is clear that practical completion is some way away, write to the contractor (Fig 6.13) informing him that you do not intend to make any more special visits in response to his requests and you will deal with completions on your normal site inspections. Whatever you do, do not give in to pressure. At the end of the day, it is your certificate and you are responsible for it.

Fig 6.13

Letter from architect to contractor if works are alleged to have achieved practical completion

Dear Sir

[*Heading*]

In response to your letter of the [*insert date*] informing me that the above works have achieved practical completion, I visited site this morning and carried out an inspection.

In my opinion, practical completion has not yet been achieved. Among the items outstanding are:

[*List some of the items you noticed*]

The above is not a comprehensive list. It is for you to ensure that the works are completed in accordance with the contract.

Abortive inspections are a waste of my time. Additional fees are chargeable which the employer would certainly seek to recover from you. I do not intend to make any further special visits in this respect. I will deal with the matter of practical completion on one of my regular site visits.

Yours faithfully

6.9 Defects liability period

It is important to remember that the defects liability period in any contract is there to enable the contractor to return to site and correct defects. If the period was not provided, the contractor would have no right to return and the client could simply take action for damages. Therefore, the end of the defects liability period does not signal the end of the contractor's liability for defects. Any defects which appear after the end of the period can be the subject of a legal action. In practice, most reasonable contractors welcome the opportunity to be able to correct defects themselves because it costs them less money than paying damages.

You must follow the contract provisions precisely. The client has the right, under some contracts, to opt not to have defects corrected and to deduct the appropriate value from the contract sum. If the employer wishes to use this option, you must be sure to obtain clear instructions from him (Fig 6.14).

Some contractors, and even some forms of contract, refer to the 'maintenance period'. The term is misleading and it should never be used because it suggests an obligation to keep the works in pristine condition rather than an obligation to correct defects.

6.10 Determination

Under the general law, a very serious breach of contract by one of the parties may entitle the other party to treat the contract as at an end. The difficulty lies in deciding when the breach is sufficiently serious. As a rough guide, it may be justified for one of the parties to terminate the contract if the other party shows that it has no intention of proceeding with the contract. There are many problems and it is not suggested that you should ever contemplate advising the client to bring the contract to an end in this way. Before taking such action the advice of a good contracts lawyer should be obtained.

Most standard forms of contract contain some provision for either party to determine the contractor's employment under the contract provided that certain conditions are satisfied. The conditions to be satisfied often fall far short of the sort of serious breaches of contract necessary for bringing the contract to an end under the general law. If you or the client (as the case may be) operate the provisions, great care must be taken that:

o The conditions for determination are satisfied *and*
o The procedure is followed exactly.

This is one instance when it pays to be pedantic. If the contract stipulates notice to be given by registered post, do just that, delivery by hand will not

Fig 6.14

Letter from architect to client if some defects are not to be made good

Dear Sir

[*Heading*]

I understand that you do not require the contractor to make good the following defects:

[*List the defects that the client does not require making good*]

These defects are included in my schedule of defects issued to the contractor at the end of the defects liability period. I am firmly of the opinion that such defects should be made good by the contractor. If you insist that such defects are not to be made good, I formally disclaim any responsibility for the consequences of whatever nature and whenever they occur and I should be pleased if you would confirm the following:

1. You do not require the contractor to carry out making good to the defects listed in this letter.

2. You authorise me to make an appropriate deduction from the contract sum.

3. You waive any rights you may have against any persons in regard to the items listed as defects in the above-mentioned schedule of defects and not made good.

4. You agree to indemnify me against any claims made by third parties arising from such defects.

Yours faithfully

suffice. If you are required to give a number of days' notice, allow the full number of days to elapse. If the client attempts determination one day early, it will be invalid and the contractor will have a case for unlawful repudiation of the contract. Seven days' notice means that the notice expires on the ninth day. If the contract states that the 'employer' (the client) is to give notice, it is not sufficient for you to give the notice.

Remember that it is the contractor's employment and not the contract itself which is ended under the provisions of most forms of contract. This is to avoid any dispute regarding whether the effect of all other clauses is removed with the determination. Carefully ensure that all the subsequent provisions are put into effect. The contract should provide that the contractor must relinquish possession of the site. The client may have the right to make use of plant on the site to complete the work and to take over contracts for the supply of work and/or materials. Usually, it will be worthwhile taking up these rights. The client may also be entitled to deduct loss and/or expense due to the determination from any future payment. Not all contracts contain this provision so check. In general, the client is not required to make any further payment to the contractor until the project has been completed by another contractor and the accounts settled up, no matter how long that may take. Among legitimately chargeable client's costs will be extra professional fees probably occasioned by the determination and subsequent new tendering and contract procedures.

Do everything in your power to prevent determination by the contractor. He may well be able to claim, not only the costs of determination, but also the profit he would have gained had the contract proceeded. Danger areas which can provoke determination by the contractor are:

o   Client's failure to pay the full amount shown in certificates within the period allowed.

o   Suspension of the work.

Remind the client of his obligation to pay on time and the consequences of failure. This is best done at the beginning of the work before or at the same time as you issue your first certificate (Fig 6.15). Try to anticipate circumstances which may cause the works to be suspended. Suspension can take place for all kinds of silly reasons such as failure to obtain planning permission in time, lack of information, meeting unsuspected underground services, etc. On the other hand, suspension can result from fire consuming all or part of the works. Never simply issue an instruction postponing the work. At the very least, give a full explanation. Far better, arrange a meeting at which both contractor and client are present and try to agree a mutually satisfactory course of action. It may involve some additional payment to the contractor, but if it precludes his determination, it could be worth while. The contractor does not benefit from suspension of works, quite the reverse, and he is probably reluctant to determine his employ-

Fig 6.15

Letter from architect to client reminding him of obligations with regard to payment

Dear Sir

[*Heading*]

In accordance with my duties under the Conditions of Contract, clause [*insert clause number*], I enclose my first interim certificate of payment due to the contractor.

This is probably an opportune time to emphasise that you have a maximum of [*insert number*] days from the date of this certificate in which to get your payment to the contractor. In the present instance, you have until [*insert date*] by which to pay.

The importance of paying the contractor the full amount indicated on the certificate within the period allowed cannot be stressed too much. Failure to honour certificates within the time limit allows the contractor to commence the procedure for determining his employment. The result of this would be disastrous to the contract in terms of both time and money.

Yours faithfully

ment if another reasonable way of arranging matters is proposed. However, you cannot expect him to lose money with a smile on his face.

6.11 Settling up

Many architects seem to leave the calculation of the final account entirely in the hands of the quantity surveyor. In most instances, the results are entirely satisfactory. If, however, you want to make a name for yourself as an effective project architect, you should involve yourself in the process. The best way to do this is to insist on checking through the material provided by the contractor. You may spot errors, particularly in regard to work carried out, which evade the quantity surveyor. Make sure that the quantity surveyor has a full set of the instructions you have issued during the course of the work and, if you have the slightest doubt, ask him to explain how he has calculated sums of money.

The quantity surveyor will usually provide you with a summary of the final account, but that alone will be insufficient to provide an adequate check. When you send the final account to the client for information before you issue the final certificate, it should be straightforward, clear and brief. Do not simply send the quantity surveyor's final account. Rearrange it so that the client can see what has occurred and the cause of any overspending. If the final sum is greater than expected, do not make the mistake of being apologetic about it. Unless you have been particularly careless, he is getting what he paid for. If you feel guilty, it will show. Be open and honest and the client will have no complaints (Fig 6.16).

6.12 Feedback

Feedback is important to you. It tells you how your building actually performs in use and whether your procedures are adequate.

It is a good idea to send a questionnaire to your client about a year after practical completion. He should appreciate that you are concerned about your work and anxious to constantly improve it. A sample questionnaire is shown in Fig 6.17, but you should devise a questionnaire suited to your own requirements and the particular building.

Always look into any complaints from the client even if you know that he is misunderstanding the purpose of some aspect of his building. If the investigation is going to take much time, you should make it clear that fees will be payable. If complaints are left unanswered, the client may decide that his solicitor should deal with the matter and a simple point may turn into major litigation. At the slightest hint of litigation, inform your insurers and consult your own solicitor.

Fig 6.16
Statement of final account to client

```
Contract sum                              £

Deduct Contingencies                      £

Add Sundry additional works
      (brief details)                     £_____

                                          £

Deduct [or Add] Adjustment of PC and
           provisional sums               £_____

                                          £

Deduct [or Add] Adjustment of
           measured work                  £_____

                                          £

Add Fluctuations                          £_____

                                          £

Add Contractor's claims for loss and/
      or expense under clause[.........]  £_____

Final amount                              £_____
```

Fig 6.17
Feedback questionnaire – example

```
Contract:                        Date:

Client:

Date of Practical Completion:
```

Please tick the appropriate box.

1. Do you consider that the brief you gave was
   completely accurate in the light of your current
   use of the building?

   Yes ☐

   No ☐

2. If no, could the discrepancy have been avoided?

   Yes ☐

   No ☐

3. From your point of view, were communications
   good throughout the design and construction
   stages?

   Yes ☐

   No ☐

4. Were the monthly financial statements clear?

   Yes ☐

   No ☐

5. Is maintenance easy?   Yes ☐

   No ☐

6. Are any of the materials used unsatisfactory?

   Yes ☐

   No ☐

Fig 6.17 – *contd.*

7. Are all the services easy to operate and
   maintain?

   Yes ☐

   No ☐

8. Are there any particular problems?

   Yes ☐

   No ☐

9. Have you any suggestions how improvements could
   be made to the service you received?

   Yes ☐
   (please
   enlarge)

   No ☐

10. Do you consider that a further review in a
    year's time would be useful?

    Yes ☐

    No ☐

When all the answers to this questionnaire have been
studied, you will be invited to attend a meeting to
discuss the points raised.

6.13   Summary

o   The clerk of works should not waste time issuing written directions.
o   The client is vicariously liable for the negligence of the clerk of works.
o   The clerk of works should not issue 'snagging lists' or deface materials on site.
o   Inspection is something done by you and the clerk of works. Supervision is carried out by the person-in-charge.
o   Never issue oral instructions.
o   The client should always authorise additional work in writing.
o   Extensions must be given for delays due to client's defaults.
o   Extensions can only be given if the contract so provides.
o   Never give reasons for your extension of time awards.
o   You can only deal with those financial claims expressly authorised by the contract.
o   When in doubt, reject claims until they are clarified.
o   The issue of the certificate of practical completion is a matter for your opinion alone. It may be issued if some very minor defects are present.
o   The defects liability period is provided for the contractor's benefit.
o   Determination may take place at common law or through the contract provisions.
o   Always avoid determination by the contractor.
o   You should understand the final account from beginning to end.
o   Send the client your own simplified version of the final account, do not simply pass on the quantity surveyor's complex calculations which may be an invitation to the employer to ask his own accountants to check.
o   A feedback questionnaire is an indication that you care.

Achieving objectives

7.1 Management

7.1.1 Definition

There are many definitions of management. Each one tries to explain what is, in effect, a simple concept. There are several very good books on the subject (see Appendix A). Although this chapter, like the rest of this book, is not concerned with theoretical discussion, an understanding of management is useful in trying to apply practical solutions to problems.

Shorn of unnecessary jargon, the purpose of management is to make the right things happen. You may consider this to be too simplistic a definition, but it should suffice for present purposes. Management is usually thought of in relation to large organisations, but it can be applied equally well to a single person. If you are in practice alone, you will have to manage your time and resources to achieve your own objectives. Much has been written about the feasibility of training people to be good managers, and one school of thought considers that good managers are born not made. Without doubting the truth of that proposition, it is also true that you can improve your management skills by absorbing a few simple techniques. On the assumption that you will eventually have to deal with staff, even if you do. not do so at present, what follows will relate to a small practice of, say, four or five people which might well exist within a larger organisation.

7.1.2 Aspects of management

There are six aspects of management which you should consider if you are to be effective in achieving your objectives:

o   Communications.
o   Objectives.
o   Leadership.
o   Motivation.
o   Delegation.
o   Authority and responsibility.

A large number of architects undoubtedly conduct their work on the basis of a ragbag of ideas and, to some extent, this approach is inevitable. A clear understanding of the above six aspects, however, will go a long way to sorting out the ragbag so that you and your group can function consistently. Inconsistency is one of the major criticisms of the management of any business. Therefore, clarify your ideas, but do not petrify them because another major criticism of management is lack of flexibility. Bear in mind that the principles hold good whether they are related to the way in which you manage yourself, the way in which you manage others or the way in which you are being managed by others.

Communications

This is the most vital aspect of management. Put simply, your ideas will be only as good as your communication of them. Do not forget that communication is a two-way street. A large proportion of problems arise during a building contract because of a failure on both sides. A message which is badly communicated to site may be poorly understood. A query on the message from the person-in-charge may be badly phrased and equally badly understood in its turn, leading to incorrect replies. Therefore, make sure that your communications are clear and learn to read the communications of others as though they have made a mistake. It is something which will improve with practice. Most people do not know how badly they convey information. If you want to test your ability, draw a simple five- or six-line diagram on a piece of paper. Try to explain the diagram to a friend so that he can draw it on his sheet of paper to the same size. The rules are that you must not let him see your paper and you must not look at his until you have finished explaining the diagram and he has finished drawing. Try the exercise two ways. One, in which he may not ask you any questions and, two, in which he can ask as many questions as he wishes until he is satisfied that he fully understands what you have drawn. Tests show that, even when questions are permitted, few people have the ability to transmit or receive this sort of information accurately. As an architect, you should be able to achieve a high degree of skill in verbal explanation of diagrams because much of the day to day business of building depends upon it.

To improve your communication skills concentrate upon the following:

o   Keep your message clear. Look at your drawings, specifications, letters and listen to what you say from the point of view of the receiver.

o   Remove ambiguities. If you mean immediately or in three days' time, say so. Do not say 'as soon as possible'. Vagueness is present in many specification clauses. Architects refer to 'best quality' or 'good quality' when they could be more precise if they took the trouble.

o   Be brief. When you have said or written down what you mean, stop. Additional words or phrases which are intended to clarify often make the communication confusing.

o   Leave nothing out. A common mistake is to make the assumption that the recipient of your message knows something of which, in fact, he is unaware.

Objectives

Failure to bear objectives in mind is a frequent source of problems in large organisations where some members of staff may have rather different objectives from those of the organisation. The problem can also occur in smaller, one-man, operations. When you take charge of your group, define your employer's and your own objectives, short and long term. Write them down and pin them up in a prominent place where you can always see them. At regular intervals, review the objectives in the light of experience. Before you perform any task, get into the habit of asking yourself if you are helping to achieve the objectives by what you are about to do. Make sure that your staff know the objectives of the practice and, on a smaller scale, the objectives with regard to any particular project.

Remember that every member of staff will have his or her own legitimate personal objectives, career advancement, for example. A good manager will be aware of these personal goals and ensure that they merge, or at least do not conflict, with the goals of the practice. If a member of staff gives you a report which has the objective of justifying his actions rather than solving the particular problem, it will be worthless, indeed it could even be damaging. Your staff will concentrate on essentials if you make it clear that you have a policy of admitting mistakes, your own included. Commiserate with one another about mistakes, then forget them and concentrate on objectives with a clear mind. Your staff will learn to take all decisions on the basis of the practice objectives and, if they make the wrong decision, they will admit it, saving time and folders of memos. Try it and you will experience team work, maybe for the first time. At the end of a year, you will be surprised at your progress.

Remember, even if objectives are clear, there may be difficulties in finding the best route to achieve them. If no trouble has been taken to define objectives in the first place, you will not even be looking for the route.

Leadership

Much rubbish has been written about leadership. To some extent, the more you try to lead the fewer followers you will have. Unless you are seeking personal honour, do not lead from the front. Work within your practice. The more inconspicuous you are, the better you will do your job. The art of leadership is to make every member of your staff think that the idea was his and then to congratulate him on it. As a leader you have only two functions:

o   Decide objectives.

o   Set the pace.

The true measure of your success is not your performance, but the performance of your staff.

Motivation

There are two distinct aspects to motivation:

o   How you motivate yourself.

o   How you motivate others.

Your motives for setting up in practice are discussed in section 9.1. The desire to be in charge of your own future or to produce your own type of architecture must be strong for you to take the plunge. Sustaining your drive after the first few months or years, perhaps when you have achieved some kind of security, may be a more difficult task. What if you are not in practice on your own, but working for a practice? Without a strong motive, you will achieve little. To maintain your own drive you must regularly sit down and consider what you want from life. Is is fame, fortune, satisfaction or something else? Keep reminding yourself. If you are in practice on your own account, your personal motives will be closely identified with your practice objectives.

Motivating others is a more difficult proposition. Your own motives can be quite different from those of your staff. They may be interested primarily in making enough money to live. Generally, motivators can be seen as achievement, recognition and advancement. Whether a particular individual acts in particular circumstances depends largely upon whether he can see that his action will result in the outcome he desires. In motivating others, therefore, it is crucial to let them see that their actions are achieving the desired end. There is no overall approach which you can apply to every individual. It is necessary to study their needs and aspirations. Like leadership, motivation is best operated unobtrusively. In essence, motivation of others consists of getting them to do what you want because they want to do it. The carrot is far more effective than the stick. The golden rules for motivating others can be summed up as follows:

o   Find out what they want.

o   Show them how they can get it by doing what you want.

o   Ensure that they are not disappointed through your fault.
o   Stand back or you will be knocked over in the rush.

Delegation
Few people know how to delegate. The principal rule is to delegate work
to the least qualified/paid person who can do the work. By giving
responsibility you encourage people to take responsibility. Too many
architects in control of staff are reluctant to delegate because they think
that the job will not be carried out properly. What they really mean is
that the job will not be carried out in precisely the way they would have
done it. Very often it will be carried out more efficiently. Take an
example: A financial claim may land on your desk. If the project is
important, you may feel that you should deal with the claim yourself
even though you have a project architect for that particular contract.
But if you delegate the job, you can be certain that it will receive the sort
of thorough attention that you will be unlikely to be able to give it. What
you should do is to hand the claim to your project architect. Tell him
that he will be dealing with it and whatever he agrees you will back. If
the contractor telephones you about the claim, tell him that you are not
dealing with it and refer him to the project architect. The result will be
that the project architect will appreciate the confidence you have placed
in him and he will spend long hours, some of them in his own time, to
make sure that he does the best possible job. You will be freed to devote
your time to work which only you can do.
If you are in a position to delegate work, your main task is to do just
that, pick the right person and give him his head. Meanwhile, see to it
that you free him from silly little jobs which prevent him from getting on
with the real work.

Authority and responsibility
The two go together. If you give someone, or someone gives you, responsibility, the appropriate authority must run alongside. Similarly, if you
are given authority in some area, you will be responsible for failure. The
point is too little appreciated. If you set up a team to do a job, you must
appoint a leader and make clear that he has the authority to organise the
work in his own way. It is no good interfering yourself and then trying to
blame him if work is not produced on schedule.
All the aspects of management discussed above are closely related. If
you have managerial responsibility, check that you are operating efficiently. If you are being managed, use the information to see how well
those above you are doing their jobs. If they are seriously defective, it is
time to move.

7.1.3 Some management techniques

It is not essential to learn any formal management techniques in order to manage efficiently. Some people are put off by the very words 'management technique' while others shelter behind them as a substitute for doing something really worth while. If the words offend you, think of them as 'a few things you can do to help keep your work moving along'. There are, of course, hundreds of things you can do and a good many of them are documented in great detail in standard management books. The purpose of this section is to mention just a few techniques which might prove useful and which, even if you never put them into operation, you should know all about.

Management by exception
Using this system, the manager only wishes to know the problems. The idea is that when he delegates work to members of his staff, they do not report back to him unless there is a problem. While things are going well, they simply get on with the job and if no one reports to him, the manager can safely assume that all projects are proceeding smoothly. Of course, in practice, the system needs a little more refinement. The people being managed must be told about the system. They must see how much time is saved by not reporting successes only failures. They must have clearly defined objectives.

Although this technique is sometimes criticised because it gives the manager a one-sided and rather bleak view of activities, it is infinitely to be preferred to the usual situation where staff rush to tell the manager about each successful accomplishment of an objective while seeking to hide failures. This latter situation is most like the position in too many offices. Remember, if you decide to operate management by exception, you and your staff must be ruthless in observing the rules. The temptation to share, with the whole office, the successful handling of a contract negotiation may be overwhelming, but you must keep your satisfaction to yourself. Of course, you may argue that this style of management takes away all the pleasure in doing the work. If that is the way you feel, you will chose some other way of managing.

Management by objectives
Before you can put this method into practice, you must know your objectives, for the firm and for the individual. The method lends itself better to some jobs than others.

If we assume that you are to do the managing, the first thing you must do is to identify the objectives to be achieved by each member of staff in turn. The best way to do this is to let each person actually agree their own objectives. If, for example, you are co-ordinating a design team, you will have produced a programme on which you have made some indication of the work to be done by various members of the team. See each member and discuss his individual programme. In simple terms, they each will agree to carry out a task within a set time limit. The really important point is that each member has set his own objectives. You must check progress regularly with the team member concerned. This means that you must take care that the objectives are broken down into manageable time periods. The advantages are that:

o   Each person has created his own pressure to get the work done on time.

o   You can check progress easily and identify problems.

The big disadvantage is the time you must take to agree objectives with the team members. In practice, the system should save time by removing possible areas of uncertainty. Every person should know exactly what he has to do.

A word of warning. The system is sometimes referred to as 'management by results' because, in some places, it is used primarily as a method of assessing the performance of staff. While there is no doubt that the system does have this capability, if you make this its prime function, you will be unlikely to receive whole-hearted co-operation. If you are a member of a design team and are asked to set your own objectives, make absolutely sure that you are realistic. The temptation is always to agree to try and do more than is really possible.

Reporting by responsibility

This technique attempts to clarify and limit the movement of information. It is probably of doubtful value in the really small office. In principle, it works like this: If A is responsible to B and B is responsible to C, then A reports to B only, never to C. C relies totally on B reporting as necessary. The great advantage is that, if properly organised, the system prevents duplication of information. In large offices, much time is wasted because people tend to copy memos, reports, etc., to everyone who might have an interest. This technique aims to control such practices by imposing clear channels of communication throughout the office. Everyone gets information strictly on what is commonly called a 'need to know' basis. The result should be that every member of the practice can be confident that all the paper that lands on his desk will be strictly relevant to his own responsibilities.

Job evaluation

A technique which attempts to ensure that a post is given the correct level of pay compared with all other posts in the practice. There are two stages:

Fig 7.1
Grading table for architectural staff (from *The Architect and his Office*)

Type of work which can be handled	Knowledge and initiative	Influence on others	Responsibility
'A' level Perform simple jobs offering little or no alternative methods. Simple analysis of problems for which logical answers are readily obtainable.	No initiative required.	Able to understand and execute simple instructions. A minimum influence on the work of others.	Responsible for making minor decisions. All work closely supervised.
'B' level Perform work offering a limited number of alternative methods. Solve problems for which logical answers are not readily apparent and which will have some effect on the other aspects of the job.	Limited initiative required. Limited research into common technical literature required. Knowledge of the more common types of materials.	Able to understand and execute instructions covering a limited field. Able to give simple clear instructions.	Responsible for making decisions affecting his work only, which must be reported to his senior. Parts of his work closely supervised.
'C' level Perform work offering a variety of alternative methods. Solve problems for which answers are not apparent and which will have considerable effect on other aspects of the job.	Initiative is required. Considerable research into all technical literature required. General knowledge of all types of materials.	Able to understand and execute instructions, covering a wide field. Able to give instructions to allocate work among and to control the work of, up to 5 or 6 others working as a team and to co-ordinate their activities.	Responsible for making decisions for all the work of his team within the framework laid down. Receives general supervision.
'D' level Perform work offering an infinite variety of alternative methods. Solve problems for which considerable thought is required to produce logical answers, the solution to which will have a profound effect on the whole design.	Considerable initiative is required. Considerable basic research is required into fields not normally covered by normal technical literature. Wide detailed knowledge of all types of materials.	Able to initiate a plan of working and check progress, able to convert plan into a practical method of working and to give the necessary instructions. Able to control and co-ordinate the work of a number of teams working independently.	Responsible for submitting and agreeing design policy with the principal within the framework laid down by the office. Receives administrative supervision only.

o   Give all posts a rank order.

o   Put salaries to the posts.

The advantages claimed for job evaluation are that it:

o   Produces a comprehensible pay structure within the practice.

o   Produces a comprehensible level of pay compared with posts out-side the practice.

o   Creates a system for fixing rates of pay for new posts.

o   Gives the employees a sense of security from arbitrary changes in salary structure.

In very large organisations, the system of job evaluation may be carried out on a points system. It is easier to do if most of the jobs being carried out are in the category of manual work. Points are awarded for various aspects of the work such as effort, skill and working conditions. It is obviously more difficult to grade the work done by professionals because much time is spent apparently doing invisible work (i.e., thinking) and the end result is not easily quantified like products off an assembly line. Small organis-ations may evaluate jobs on an instinctive basis. It is important to remem-ber that it is the post and not the individual which is being evaluated by this technique. Of interest to the architectural office is the survey *The Architect and his Office* which was carried out in 1961. Posts were evaluated on four levels which included all architectural staff except principals (Fig 7.1).

It is unlikely that you will be involved in very detailed job evaluation whether as principal or participant. In either case, you will be wise to keep a very close watch on salaries being advertised for similar posts in other practices so that you can be sure that they are comparable to what you are offering/getting. Do not expect precise correlations because the circum-stances and duties of professional posts can be very variable.

Cost-effectiveness

Shorn of all jargon, cost-effectiveness is simply the art of ensuring that, consistent with the job being done satisfactorily, all jobs are carried out:

o   In the cheapest possible way.

o   By the lowest paid member of staff.

To take a simple example: if the job is to take letters to the post, they may be taken by car or they may be taken on foot. They may be taken by the principal or by the officer junior. Provided the post office is relatively near, it will be cheaper to take the letters on foot. All things being equal, it will be cheaper for the office junior to take them than the principal. Particular circumstances can alter the equation, of course. If the principal is about to go home and the office junior is busy with something else, it might be cheaper, overall, if the principal dropped the letters in at the post office on the way home. If you always ensure that jobs are carried out by the cheapest route in terms of both method and manpower, you will be said to be cost-effective. Where a great deal of money is at stake and complex factors are operating, estimates should be made of the various ways of accomplishing the task. Provided that each way will result in a satisfactory accomplishment, the cheapest should be chosen. The application of the principle to architectural practice may seem to be either obvious or unnecessary. The important thing is to remember the principle. Too often, jobs in an office are done by the most highly paid person capable of doing them and they are carried out in the most expensive way possible. If you think that is a bleak view, consider the number of offices that do not attempt to be cost-effective when preparing production drawings. The architect often attempts to do things in the best possible way without giving too much thought to whether there is a cheaper way to do them.

The 80/20 rule

This is one of those empiric rules which can be seen to apply in a large number of situations although there appears to be no hard scientific reason. Basically, the rule states that over a spectrum of activities or products, etc., the return will not equal the effort, but will be proportioned approximately in the ratio 80/20. Thus, if you have a large number of clients, 20% will account for 80% of your income. Therefore, 80% of your clients will account for only 20% of your income. The rule becomes more accurate, the greater the number and variety of people or items being considered. The rule was formulated after a considerable amount of fieldwork and appears to hold up across a wide variety of situations. Its application is probably most useful in product marketing. If a factory produces a range of goods, 20% of them will account for 80% of the value. If you are in practice, test the rule. It can tell you something about your workload and suggest ways in which you should improve your marketing strategy.

Bring forward system

This is a technique for dealing with correspondence. In many offices, the problem with letters is two-fold:

o   Incoming mail is retained by individuals, perhaps pending reply, the correspondence files are permanently out of date and there is serious danger that the original letter may be lost.

o   There is no effective follow up for outgoing letters requiring a reply.

The 'bring forward' or 'call back' system makes use of coloured postcards and requires the assistance of a typist, filing clerk or secretary. It is not really possible to operate it on an individual basis, the whole office must

Fig 7.2

Example of the layout of a typical 'bring forward' card

Bring forward on:	5·6·86	17·6·86		

Return to: David Chappell

File Ref: 21/17

Letter to/from: Eager Builders

Dated: 28·5·86

be involved. It works like this: You receive a letter through the office system. The letter requires a reply, but you are unable to reply immediately either because you are busy with something else or you need further information or for some other reason. You decide when you will be able to deal with the letter, enter the details on the coloured post-card, pin it to the letter and send immediately to filing. An example of the type of card you could use is shown in Fig 7.2. The important point about the card is that it should be easy and quick to complete. The person responsible for filing puts the letter in the correspondence file with the rest and sticks your card in a small desk file. All such cards are filed in order of the date on which you wish to deal with the letter. The filing clerk, or whoever is designated to do the job, looks at the card file every morning. On the date you decided to deal with the letter, the card and the complete file is laid on your desk for attention. If you can answer the letter, you do so, throwing away the card. If you are still unable to answer the letter, decide on a new date and insert it, crossing out the old then go through the process again.

The system can be used if you are writing letters. Frequently you will write to someone expecting an answer or some action. If you complete a card when you write your letter, you can ensure that on a particular date of your choice the file and your card is brought back to you so that you can check that you have had some response. The essence of the system lies in the cards being simple to complete and the person responsible for filing and retrieving them being totally reliable. When the system is operated efficiently, it has many benefits:

o   Correspondence files are always complete.

o   Your pending tray is not piled high with letters to be answered some time in the future.

o   There is no need to retain copies of your own letters to ensure a follow up.

o   You will be well organised and, therefore, save time.

7.2   Decision making

7.2.1 Problem solving

The making of any decision should involve the principles which follow. It is not suggested that you should laboriously go through the method outlined step by step for every problem you encounter, but if you study the principles thoroughly, following the procedure should become so much a part of your professional life that you will not consciously think about it. When you have to make a decision, it will be because there is a problem. Many of the decisions you make in order to answer the problems you face will be minor ones, but interwoven with other decisions so that the whole appears impossibly complicated. The first thing to do is to isolate the various decisions you have to make so that you can consider them one by one. Some decisions will affect other decisions, others will simply affect an isolated part of your work. The decision to be made first is the one which affects most other decisions.

Decide whether a particular decision is of major or minor importance. This will determine the amount of time you should spend on it. There is absolutely no point whatever in agonising over a decision that has very little implication, even if it is wrong. This is probably the most important stage in the decision-making process and you must give it enough thought.

Make sure you know the problem. Do not act like the students in an examination who often answer the question that is not asked. One thing you should ask yourself is 'Is it my problem?' Very often architects, being generally helpful souls, put themselves to endless trouble solving other peoples' problems without really understanding that they can stand back and let the client, contractor, consultant (delete as appropriate) answer it. Assuming that you identify the problem as one which you must deal with, write it down in as few words as possible. The act of writing will help to clarify the matter you are to consider.

7.2.2 Ordering

The next stage is to examine every aspect of the problem. Write down as a series of notes all the implications, time-scale, financial, physical, special conditions, side-effects on other actions, etc. After writing down everything you can think of, do some research among documents (drawings, bills of quantities, etc.), colleagues, publications and on site if appropriate. Go through your list combining items which are linked and crossing out duplications. Then prepare another list by going through your notes and identifying the most important consideration and putting it at the top. Carry on until you have rewritten all the points in order of importance. You now have the criteria for your decision in order.

Take another sheet of paper and, using the points from your first sheet, note down as many possible solutions as you can. Do not worry at this stage if some of the solutions seem impracticable. When you have listed all the possible solutions, examine each in turn against your list of criteria and note the results as a schedule. The schedule should show the good and bad results of each possible solution in each area. It should be possible to eliminate some possible solutions immediately.

7.2.3 Making the decision

Armed with a sheet of paper listing the problem and its consequences, side-effects and implications in every way and another sheet listing possible solutions analysed against the first sheet, you are in a position to come to a decision. Since you can only arrive at one decision, you should strike out any solution that clearly does not satisfy the criteria. You should be left with two or three solutions which appear equally well suited to the problem. Often you will simply be left with one solution which, after this analysis, shines out clearly above all the rest.

If you do find that two solutions appear to be equally good, examine them carefully to see if one is slightly better in some respect not hitherto considered. If that fails to produce a best solution, you can choose either one. Fig 7.3 shows a decision flow chart.

7.2.4 Problems in decision making

At the end of the process you may find that there is nothing you can do to solve the problem adequately. That is rare. There is a solution to most problems. Consider all the options again. More common is that no solution solves the problem as adequately as you would wish. If you cannot find another solution, you must use the best solution you have.

Never rush a decision. You will save no time by doing so because your decision under pressure is unlikely to be as good as it could be. There are two questions which you can ask yourself when trying to decide between two courses of action:

o   What should I *not* do?

o   If my decision is wrong, what is the worst thing that could happen?

Fig 7.3
Flow chart – making a decision

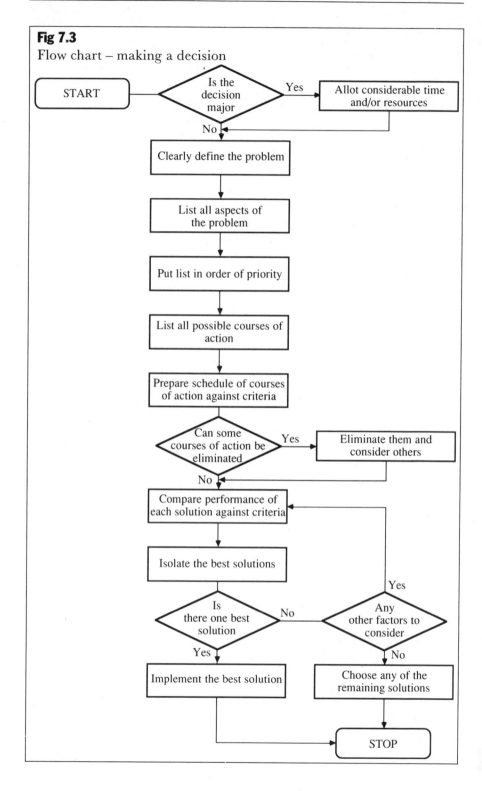

7.3   Organising time

7.3.1 The approach

Do not fall into the trap of spending so much time organising your time that you have little time left over for your real work. It is an easy mistake to make. Organising time is like any other business activity; when the disadvantages begin to equal the advantages, it is time to stop.

Basically, organisation of time is worth while because an organised person can achieve more and suffer less stress in the process than someone to whom things just 'happen'.

You may find it easiest to organise yourself in easy stages. Unless you are already a pretty well-organised person, a complete change in your method of working may give you such an unpleasant shock that you relapse quite quickly into former attitudes.

The first stage is to think about the tasks that you must do during the next month. Write them down. Divide the month into weeks and decide which task should be done in which week and, indeed, which tasks will spread over more than one week. Write them down and divide the first week into days and allocate the tasks again. These should be your major work, around which you must arrange everything else that you have to do. For example, your tasks might include such things as writing a report, preparing a sketch design, making a certain number of visits to site, etc. Some of these activities will have built-in deadlines; if not, make your own deadline. When thinking about your work always move from the important to the less important and from the general to the particular. Make sure you know the wood before you begin to count the trees.

It might help if you make yourself a *brief* programme indicating, week by week, major tasks for a month ahead and major tasks on a day by day basis for the first week (see Fig 7.4).

Obviously, you must keep a diary. Some people prefer the type which gives the week at a glance, but if you really want to keep track of everything, you need a diary that devotes a page to each day. Diary entries fall into two categories:

o   Planning – things to do, people to see, etc.

o   Recording – things done, people seen, etc.

It is possible to buy or produce diaries which are especially arranged to assist this division and othe divisions too. On the whole, however, the simpler the approach, the more chance there is that you will stick to it.

Always keep your diary open, with a clip on the page, as a silent reminder. At the beginning of each week, or at the end of the previous week, plan your tasks as indicated above. Transfer the information to your diary and you can be sure that you will miss out nothing that is important. All the

Fig 7.4
Programming on a monthly basis – major tasks

Week 1	Week 2	Week 3	Week 4
Feasibility for Country Club	Examine Eeger Builder's claim	Factory sketch design	Sketch design presentation to client
L.A. re. Factory	Settle outstanding QS queries on Motor Showrm.	Collate office manual with Ken	See ministry man re. Hsg. Estate
Survey at Hall's Well			
Seminar on IFC 84	Defects inspection at Sauri Estate	Practical Com. at Thrum?	Deadline for Art Gallery Comp.
Site visits: Thrum, Poodges, Purrock.	SV: Thrum, Poodges, Purrock.	SV: Thrum, Poodges, Purrock (special meeting)	SV: Thrum, Poodges, Purrock.

Day 1	Day 2	Day 3	Day 4	Day 5
L.A. re. Factory	Visit Poodges site	Seminar IFC 84 (all day)	Visit Thrum site	Feasibility
Hall's Well survey	Hall's Well survey		Visit Purrock site	

other smaller things which you have to do will then be planned around the major tasks.

7.3.2 Practical hints

o   Organise the day into blocks of work (see Fig 7.5). Do not try to plan every minute. Leave spare time. Star the priorities or write in red ink.

o   Cut out after-hours working as soon as possible. Everyone has to do some work after normal working hours from time to time, but do not make it a permanent feature of your life or you will become permanently tired and unable to attack your work with the vigour it requires. You will also make more mistakes.

o   Use your time effectively. Fig 7.6 shows the situation in the form of a flow chart. Do not dither. If you can do something that needs doing, do it, if not identify the reason and set in motion the means whereby you will be able to tackle the problem.

o   Use your skills effectively. It is tempting to waste time on unimportant matters just because they are your particular interest. If you do, you will lack the energy to do the jobs which really matter.

o   Keep meetings to a minimum. This includes appointments. Ask yourself if they are really necessary. Do they help you achieve the firm's objectives? (see section 7.1.2). You are too busy to waste time – so are other people.

o   Allocate some time each week to read journals. Learn to read only those parts that are strictly relevant to your work. You *must* be up to date in every facet of your profession. As a simple guide, if you enjoy reading the weekly and monthly magazines, your are wasting too much time on them. If you like to spend time on particular journals, do it at home and treat it as relaxation.

7.4   How to be effective

7.4.1 Expansion

Many people say that if you do not expand, you contract. This can frighten you if you have just set up your own practice. You may find that you are running around in circles going nowhere. You are more likely to come to grief by expanding too rapidly so that your commitments outstrip your resources. Decide whether you want to expand or whether you are happiest as you are. Learn to separate good advice from ill-founded saws.

Fig 7.5

Example of day organised into blocks with time left free

0830   Correspondence

0900   Factory sketch design*

0930

1000

1030

1100

1130

1200   Fire Prevention Officer

1230   Return calls

1300   ⎤
        ⎥   Lunch
1330   ⎦

1400   See consultant re. offices*

1430   Prepare Eeger Builders contract

1500

1530

1600

1630

1700   Return calls

1730

Fig 7.6

Flow chart – effective use of time

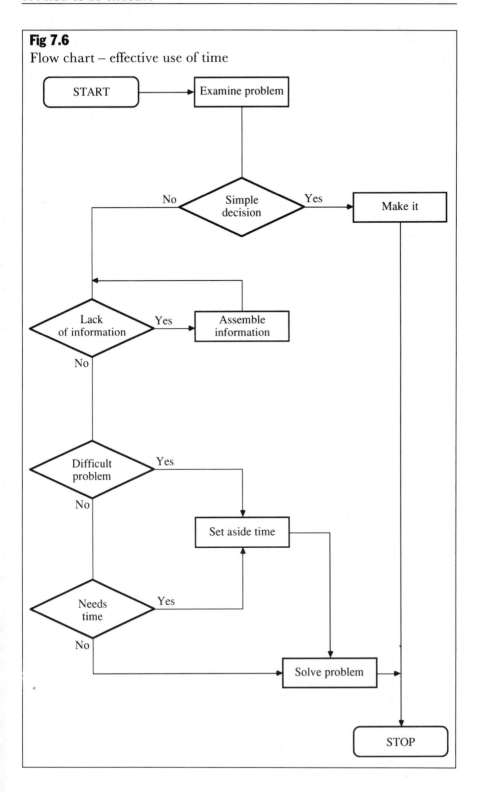

7.4.2 Priorities

Every day look at your diary and decide which task you least want to do, it may be producing a report or telephoning a client with bad news. Do it first. You may be pleasantly surprised. More important, you will have rid yourself of that terrible feeling of apprehension for the rest of the day.

7.4.3 Good ideas

Everyone has a good idea at some time or other. If you get one and put it to your principal, do not be surprised if he shows no enthusiasm. Provided only that you are convinced that your idea is valid, persevere in your efforts to convince others. Resistance often indicates no more than an unwillingness to change old habits. If you can show what your idea will mean in money terms you can convince anyone. The profit motive is strong even in the most generous of people. If a colleague or a member of your staff gets an idea, make him prove that it is good. You may lose some good ideas, but you should gain resourceful staff.

7.4.4 Competent people

The trouble with really good architects is that they tend to be given all the difficult problems to solve – simply because they are good. Most architects thrive on problems, but if they are given nothing but awkward problems, they may become jaded. A good man should be nurtured and given something less stressful in between high-pressure work. If you are the one getting all the awkward jobs, try asking for a change. Everyone will get the message. If you really are good, you will get the change you want. If you meet resistance, it is time to change your job and go and work somewhere where you will be appreciated.

7.4.5 Compromising

Try not to compromise. It may well be that most things in life are the result of compromise, but then most things in life are mediocre. All the really outstanding achievements are the result of people sticking to their ideas despite opposition.

If your client dislikes your proposal and asks you to modify it, ask yourself 'Is he right?' If he is, you will, of course modify accordingly. If he is wrong, if you are sure you are right, stand firm. He will thank you later or, if he does not actually thank you, you will not get the criticism from him that a compromise inevitably attracts.

7.5   Summary

o   Management is simply making the right things happen.

o   Remember that communication is a two-way street.

o   Know your objectives and those of the practice.

o   Leadership is not conspicuous.

o   Take the trouble to find out what motivates others.

o   Delegate wholeheartedly or not at all.

o   Authority and responsibility are like Siamese twins – difficult, if not impossible, to separate.

o   Every person with authority uses management techniques whether they know it or not.

o   Making a decision involves self-discipline.

o   Organising your time consists of organising your tasks.

o   Always keep your diary open.

o   Always have some spare time.

o   Do not work after hours on a regular basis.

o   Do not waste time on the unimportant simply because it is interesting – remember your objectives.

Climbing the ladder

Architects are not generally admired for their managerial or organisational prowess. It is difficult to see why this should be so. The skills of analysis, synthesis, problem identification and problem solving which the architect brings to the task of taking a project from brief to completion, demonstrate a high degree of organisational ability.

The working life of most architects falls into two parts:

o   Professional work.
o   Managerial work.

It is usual for the managerial function to increase at the expense of the professional function as the architect progresses to increasingly senior positions. The most senior position to which you can aspire is to be the principal or partner in your own practice. In this situation, you have total responsibility for the office, the work produced, the welfare of the staff and the very survival of the business.

Even in the present economic climate, new practices are being formed. There is all the difference in the world between being a senior architect in an office and actually running the office to make a profit. Chapter 9 deals briefly with setting up in practice, but this chapter looks at the mechanics of working your way up through the practice.

8.2   Staying or moving

Working your way up through a practice is a time-honoured way of becoming a partner in your own practice. The idea is that you join a practice whose work you admire. You work very hard, over and above the call of duty. It is to be hoped that your talents and devotion to the practice are recognised and you make no serious mistakes. In time, perhaps to dissuade you from leaving to join another practice, you are made an associate. Some years and much hard work later, you are invited to become a partner.

The advantage with this system is that you should be taking home a reasonable and increasing salary during the whole of the time you are employed by the practice until you become a partner. You will get to know the working of the office, the clients, the jobs and, most important, your colleagues.

The big disadvantage is that you may spend several years achieving the position of associate and then discover that you are destined to progress no further in that particular firm. You may then be faced with the prospect of joining another firm and going through a somewhat similar, if shortened, process if you wish to attain partner status.

You cannot expect an employer to guarantee you eventual partnership at the time you join, so the procedure is something of a gamble. Having said that, it is reasonable for you to expect a partnership at some time in the future if you are prepared to work hard. Employers are not generally fools, otherwise they would not stay in business long, and good hard work is usually rewarded. The chances are, of course, that there will be other members of the firm with the same idea as you.

If you are looking to become a partner eventually, and not everyone has that ambition, or if you are simply hopeful of achieving a senior position, such as associateship, within a practice, from time to time you will have to decide whether you should stay where you are or move to another office. If you do decide that your career requires you to move, never change your mind and stay on simply because you are offered a rise in salary. There are many architects who have postponed a move for this reason once, twice or many times, but it is never worthwhile in the end. There will come a time when you are no longer offered more money if you agree to stay and that time will undoubtedly coincide with your inability to secure the kind of post you want elsewhere.

If you are offered the chance of real advancement within the firm, that could be a good reason for staying. Beware, however; such promises are not always kept. A written undertaking that in x years you will be considered for a partnership is what you are looking for. After x years, you must find out the position. Do not hesitate to move at that stage if you meet any prevarication.

The arguments for staying in an office can be summarised as follows:

o   You know the partners.
o   You know the other members of staff.

o   You know the clients.
o   You know the work.
o   You have a good idea of your prospects.
o   The partners know you.

You know the partners
You know their strengths and weaknesses. You have a good idea whether you could get on with them if you become a partner yourself.

You know the other members of staff
It is comparatively rare, but not unknown, for really serious differences to persist among architects in an office. It is equally rare for relationships to be on a perfect level. If you have an excellent relationship with your colleagues, it can make working a pleasure. It is not something which you may want to give up lightly. However, if you do not leave, your colleagues may. So, to miss the opportunity of an enhancing move for this reason could be a mistake.

You know the clients
Most offices have a number of clients who commission work continuously. You probably know some of them quite well. Perhaps you hold one another in mutually high regard. A good relationship with a client can prove useful if you decide to set up in practice on your own. If you work well with your clients, you may not wish to exchange that relationship for another firm with unknown and possibly difficult clients. On its own, this is not a good reason for staying.

You know the work
Every office works in a slightly different way. Some of these differences have already been highlighted in previous chapters. The longer you stay in an office, the better you understand the method of getting things done and, provided that you apply yourself, you can work the system to your best advantage. Moving to another office means learning all the little wrinkles again and it will be a little time before you can relax. This could be exactly the reason for moving. When you begin to feel comfortable, it is time for a change. Of course, if you are sufficiently self-motivated, you will never feel comfortable.
Another aspect of knowing the work is the opportunity you may have to specialise in a particular building type or professional skill, This is very much a two-edged sword. The time will come when you are so expert in your field that projects become repetitive. Instead of extending your powers by challenging your intellect, they cause you to stagnate. A move to another office, where you can continue your specialism with new projects for new clients in a new environment, can be beneficial.

You have a good idea of your prospects
If you really do know that you are to be offered big advancement within the office, that may be the best of all reasons for staying, provided that there are no other active contra-indications. Unfortunately, it is virtually impossible to be sure about such things. Some architects stay out of hope; a vague notion that they must have a better chance of promotion where they are than if they moved to another practice. Do not be one of them. When the time comes and you are considering leaving, find out exactly where you stand by asking. Never trust the nod and wink. If your employer will not give you a straight answer it is because the only answer he could truthfully give you would not be to your liking. Act accordingly.

The partners know you
This can be a powerful reason for staying. You may have built up an excellent reputation with the partners for skill at your work. Move somewhere else and, in spite of any glowing references, you have to build up a reputation again. However, it is one thing to have a good reputation with the partners, but it is quite another for them to do something about it. They may take you for granted. The only way to cure that is to move.
Do not forget that as well as knowing your strengths, the partners will also know your weaknesses. Your promotion may be being blocked because one of the partners can never forget one of your mistakes.

The arguments for moving to another office can be summarised as follows:
o   Opportunity to increase salary.
o   Opportunity to improve your status.
o   Opportunity to vary experience.
o   Chance to leave mistakes behind.

Opportunity to increase salary
Architects sometimes move to another post on the same salary. It has been known for an architect to accept a drop in salary for the chance to work in a particular office. It is usual, however, for you to get an increase when you move. It would be foolish to move to another office simply because it offered more money, but it makes sense to leave your present office if they are not paying you enough.

Opportunity to improve your status
It would be a very rare, and ill-advised, occurrence for you to move from your present firm straight to a partnership in another office. It is not common for an architect to be appointed as an associate immediately. The reason is that both situations imply a degree of esteem and trust which it is not possible to develop over the course of an interview. It is

possible, however, for you to secure an appointment at a more senior level than you presently enjoy or to be appointed to a post with the assurance that in a set number of years you will be offered a partnership, provided that all parties are satisfied. Whether you could achieve the same degree of success by staying where you are is a matter for your own judgment, depending on circumstances.

Opportunity to vary experience
This is a valid reason for moving. If you stay in one office for the whole of your career, you will develop a parochial outlook unless you are a very singular person. Even if you move from one office specialising in factories to another office specialising in factories, you will broaden your outlook.

Chance to leave mistakes behind
Everyone makes mistakes. Generally, a sensible employer will take the rough with the smooth, provided that your mistakes are not serious. If you have the misfortune to make a serious mistake, you may never live it down in that particular office. A move to a different office can be the answer. Do not move immediately. Stay to sort out the mess. You may redeem yourself. In any case, there are few things more off-putting than being called back to your old office to attend conferences with partners and solicitors. When the fuss has died away, test the temperature. If it is clear that you will never be forgiven, move.

There is no simple answer to the question: should you stay or move? You have to adopt a straightforward approach. Are you happy where you work? If not, why not? Is it the type of work, the money or the people or simply the administrative machinery that is getting you down? Is there anything you can do to correct the situation? If so, do it. If not, move. Too many architects hang on year after year, hoping that something will turn up. It won't.

8.3   Promotion

8.3.1 Senior architect

If your office employs a number of architects, it is certain that the salaries will differ, depending on skill and experience. Promotion involves not only an increase in salary, but also an increase in the level of responsibility. It is the increase in responsibility which you should be seeking. It is usual for an office to signal the fact that you have been promoted by changing your job title. You may now be called 'senior architect' or 'principal architect' or some such title. Provided that it is one of the RIBA accepted job titles, it is not very important. Prestigious-sounding titles are sometimes used to pacify people who are getting restless or looking for a rise. If you are offered an important-sounding title, ask:

o   What is your extra responsibility?

o   What is the increase in your salary?

If the answer is none or virtually none, you are being taken for a fool. Prove that you are anything but a fool by moving.

How and how soon will you achieve promotion? Assuming that you are competent and take notice of the points in this book, you should expect some kind of promotion within two or, at most, three years from taking up your post. If you are not promoted in this period, you are probably not appreciated by your practice and you should consider achieving the promotion by moving elsewhere. It may be, of course, that your office just cannot afford to promote you because business is bad. Do not be sidetracked. It still amounts to the fact that you are not promoted and you must consider moving.

To achieve promotion you must:

o   Seize opportunities to demonstrate your worth.

o   Tackle mundane tasks with efficiency.

o   Tackle important jobs with flair.

o   Constantly make suggestions to the partners for improving office efficiency.

o   Identify the objectives of the office and be single-minded in their pursuit.

o   Be enthusiastic, co-operative and self-controlled.

o   Never blame others for your mistakes.

o   Never blame others for their mistakes, concentrate on solving the problem.

8.3.2 Associate

Many practices appoint associates. An associate is not a partner and the term 'associate partner' must never be used. Serious legal consequences and liabilities may result. Associates may be appointed for a number of reasons:

o   To indicate to the public that the person is a highly trusted and valued member of staff.

o   To give recognition, short of full partnership, to a member of staff who warrants enhanced status and responsibility.

o   To demonstrate the intention of the partners to proceed towards eventual partnership.

o   To satisfy the aspirations of an able member of staff who might otherwise seek better prospects elsewhere.

It is usual to list associates on the letterhead. It must be clear that the person or persons so listed are not partners and the word 'associate' should precede any such list. The practice of separating associates from partners by listing the former at the bottom of stationery, has much to recommend it.

It is usual to appoint associates by an exchange of letters after informal discussions. Some offices insist on having a deed prepared. In any event, you should seek the advice of your own solicitor.

The difference between an associate and any other employee of a practice is a question of degree. An associate probably earns more than any one in the firm other than the partners and he may have some other perks such as the use of an office car and the practice may pay his telephone bill. Associates are sometimes expected to take a part in the formulation of office policy. Despite all this, there is one crucial difference between an associate and a partner. The associate, unlike the partner, has no liability for any debts of the partnership or any claims against the partnership. He does not share in the profits or losses of the partnership except that he may share in a bonus scheme like any other member of staff. If you are invited to become an associate, the need to differentiate your status, in the eyes of the public as well as actually, is one reason why you must take legal advice.

8.3.3 Salaried partner

It is not uncommon for some firms to enter into an agreement whereby a promising architect becomes a salaried partner. If you are in this situation, you will probably receive an annual salary plus an agreed small percentage of the profits. You may then be in one of several positions:

o   A trusted employee entitled to what amounts to an annual bonus. In this case, you may as well be called an associate.

o   A partner entitled to take part in the policy-making process of the practice, but fully indemnified by the other partners in respect of any claims made on the partnership or you personally in connection with partnerhip business.

o   A partner entitled to take part in the policy-making process of the practice and liable with the other partners for the firm's contracts or torts. Clearly, the last situation must be avoided. It is important to realise that, if your name appears on the letterheads as a partner, you will be considered as a full partner by everyone outside the partnership. It may give you a rosy feeling until someone decides to sue you.

The position of salaried partners is fraught with difficulties. Even an indemnity by the full partners may not be sufficient to save you from financial disaster if a large claim is made because:

o   The other partners may seek to find a way around the indemnity (which may be imperfectly drafted) to make you take a share of the liability.

o   The total assets of the practice, together with the total personal assets of the other partners, may be insufficient to meet a claim.

A salaried partnership for a limited period is sometimes offered as a first step towards full partnership so that the other partners can assess your worth. You should consider carefully before accepting and a proper partnership deed should be drawn up with the advice of your (not the partnership's) solicitor.

8.4   Partnership

8.4.1   What is it?

A great many practices are carried on in the form of partnerships. A partnership is governed by the Partnership Act 1890.

It is important clearly to know the nature of a partnership. It is a relationship between two or more persons carrying on a business with a view to profit. There need not even be any written agreement although it is obviously desirable. Indeed, you would be foolish to enter into a partnership without an agreement. If a case comes before the courts and there is a question as to whether there is a partnership in existence, a crucial factor is whether or not the parties share in the profits (or losses). If they do then, in general, it is a partnership.

8.4.2   Advantages and disadvantages

The advantages of a partnership are:

o   Two or more people should be able to generate more ideas and attract more work than one person alone.

o   There is more than one person with a personal interest and stake in the firm. A sole principal has no one with whom he can discuss his problems.

o   It is a very close and potentially rewarding relationship between friends who share the same aims and who have complete trust in one another.

o   There is more than one person to bear any loss.

o   There may be tax benefits.

The disadvantages of a partnership are:

o   There is unlimited liability for negligence. Each partner is responsible to the full extent of his personal assets for the debts of the partnership.

o   It is not easy to remove a partner who is not pulling his weight.
o   It is difficult to obtain capital from external sources.

8.4.3 Liability

The greatest disadvantage of a partnership is liability. It comes in two main forms:
o   Your liability for negligence.
o   Your liability for partnership debts.
Negligence can produce a debt through a successful claim for damages against your firm. Debts can also arise through normal business transactions, particularly in conditions of falling workload.
Partners are jointly and severally liable in the case of negligence and other torts. They are normally only jointly liable in the case of simple contracted debts (such as the purchase of a firm's motor car or typewriter). In the first case, the party seeking damages can choose to pursue all the partners or any combination of partners or can sue each in turn until the damages are recovered in full. In the case of a simple debt, the party seeking payment is only allowed one bite at the cherry. The difference is more apparent than real because most creditors will opt to bring the action against all the partners together. The situation can become very complicated and, if you are sued, it is essential that you obtain legal advice. The partnership agreement (see section 8.4.8) may well affect matters as between partners although it has no relevance for third parties.
It is important to remember that your liability in terms of negligence can extend to liability for the negligence of one of your partners or a member of your staff. At the time of writing, your liability for actions taken by you or other members of the firm may extend for many years. Even after your death, your estate can be used to satisfy successful negligence claims.
The actual amount of your shareholding in the partnership is unimportant if your partners cannot afford to pay. It is best illustrated by an example:
Suppose one of your partners is negligent and your client successfully sues for damages. You may be faced with a bill for several thousand pounds. If you are wise, you and your partners will have taken out professional indemnity insurance to cover the amount of any probable claim. However, the insurance cover may not be, in the event, sufficient to take care of the full amount you owe. Worse still, your insurance company may decline to pay anything because you were in default in providing them with information in good time, your disclosure was faulty or for some other reason. Your firm may be faced with a colossal bill. All your business assets must be liquidated to pay and that is the end of the firm. It is not, however, the end of your liability. If the business assets are not suf-

ficient to satisfy the debt, all the partners are liable to contribute from their personal assets in the proportion of their shareholding. If your shareholding is 10% and the debt is £100,000, you would normally be liable to pay £10,000. If your partners cannot raise the remaining £90,000 after disposing of all their assets, you are liable to make up the difference. If your partners have no assets at all, you are liable for the full £100,000.

Remember, the more you have, the more you stand to lose. You may spend thirty years building up a vast personal fortune, cars, mansions, holiday homes, etc., only to lose it all because your partner or a member of your staff is negligent. It is a most important consideration when contemplating partnership. You can be equally devastated as a sole principal, but you are not liable for the actions of any partners (because you have none) and the staff are entirely under your control. You may think it is better to be able to say 'I am paying for my own carelessness' than 'I am paying for my partner's carelessness'. Of course, it may be your partners who have to pay for your carelessness.

8.4.4 Safeguards

In a partnership, you will be open to a number of dangers over and above those faced by the sole principal. They stem from the fact that you are responsible for the actions of others. Even if you know nothing about them, you must share liability for your partner's actions' provided only that they are carried out as part of your normal everyday business. For example, your partner may negotiate with a developer and a builder to set up a land deal. You will share the burden if the venture ends in financial disaster. Your partner may be in charge of an office project and commit a terrible blunder. You must help to pick up the pieces. If your partner uses his site visits to carry out criminal activities, you will not be liable – unless, of course, you are aware of them.

Some safeguards can be written into the partnership agreement (see section 8.4.8), but remember that the agreement only defines the situation between partners. Members of the public who deal with the partnership are unaffected. Thus, in the unlikely event that your agreement states that your partner will be liable for all negligence claims, the third party may claim against you, but you will have a good claim for the total sum against your partner.

There are only two possible ways to safeguard your personal assets in the event of a successful claim against the practice in which you are a partner (ignoring professional indemnity insurance for the moment):

o   Be an employee of that firm.
o   Have no personal assets.

To be an employee of your own firm involves being a director of a limited company.

If you have no personal assets, you will not be worth suing. No one throws good money after bad. It is highly likely that, during the first years of partnership, you will have no personal assets except, perhaps, your home (which may be heavily mortgaged and, therefore, not a substantial asset). It is perfectly possible for you to have all your worldly goods in someone else's name, your wife or a close relative for example, so that they own them and you become a 'man of straw'. The advice of a good solicitor is vital if you wish to arrange your affairs in this way and you must remember that your wife may divorce you or your relative may decide to hang on to your assets and there is very little you can do about it.

There are other considerations too. You are not really a fully committed partner if you have all your assets neatly out of harm's way while your partners' assets are readily available. If you all agree to become 'men of straw', you are not taking a proper professional stance towards the outside world. Clients may decline to do business with you – though once that has been said, you should take some steps to protect yourself in today's litigious climate.

8.4.5 Some problems

The advantages of a partnership can be overestimated, the disadvantages cannot. Horror stories abound. Even if a partnership begins as a coming together of like-minded people, the passage of years and events can turn it into an uneasy coalition of individuals with grievances, ambitions, mistrust and even mutual dislike. Problems seldom occur when times are good. The testing period of any partnership (like a marriage – to which it is often likened) is when times are difficult, clients and money scarce.

You may think that if you are a partner in a firm employing ten or more staff, you will be cushioned if the workload falls – you can simply get rid of staff, saving money and thereby protecting your own income. In reality, you may find yourself taking virtually nothing out of the firm for your own drawings, so that staff can be paid in the expectation of better times around the corner. Even if you wish to take a hard line and reduce staff, your partners may be better able financially to weather the storm and may vote you down. If you have insufficient savings to carry you through, you may be the one who has to leave. That said, it is unusual for partners to force one of their number to leave due to temporary financial embarrassment if he can show himself to be a valuable asset to the firm either for his design, managerial or work-attracting talents. If you are a partner you should make sure that:

o   You build up personal savings against a rainy day which is certain to arrive when you least expect it.

o   You show yourself to be an indispensable member of the firm.

If you reach the point where you really are the firm, in other words, take you away and the firm collapses, you will be in little danger of being forced to leave, even if you have to draw money while your financially better off partners draw nothing. Indeed, if you get to this position, you will begin to ask yourself seriously if your partners are pulling their weight. You may be able to promote greater involvement by your partners or increase your share of the firm by threatening to leave. This is the severest sanction you can use, but think carefully before putting it into effect. It involves breaking up the partnership if they, unexpectedly, accept your offer. Even if you get what you want, relationships will never be the same again. Arguments between partners are inevitable. They are usually accepted as part of the business of running a firm and there are generally no lasting resentments if you are all basically good friends with implicit trust in one another.

What if your business does not succeed and you decide to call it a day? That will be the true test of a partnership; to stick together in perfect trust while trying to bring your business to a close. None of you can simply walk away and leave it. All loose ends must be carefully tidied away; and this while you are probably looking for another job. What if, in such circumstances, your partner simply disappears, emigrating to Canada with a few valuable portable assets? You will have the task of sorting out the mess, dealing with creditors, accountants solicitors and possibly irate clients and contractors.

If you did not know it already, you will have realised by now that the idealistic vision of a partnership, perhaps floated with friends as a student, is a very different thing in practice. That is not to say, of course, that there are not partnerships within which not a harsh word is ever spoken. It is up to you and your partners to ensure that yours is that kind of partnership. It entails a lot of hard work. If you are in any doubt about your ability to work in these conditions, opt for a different form of practice.

It is advisable to consider the worst that can happen and decide whether you are ready to accept the risks *before* you take on the heavy responsibilities of partnership.

8.4.6 Points to note

Numbers of partners. There is no limitation on the number of partners in a professional business, but if the number is to exceed twenty, you must apply to the Registrar of Companies for approval.

Name of firm. The firm name of a partnership will be one of the following:

○   Name consisting of the names of all the partners.

○   A name consisting of the names of some of the partners.

○   A name consisting of the names of partners who are retired or dead, possibly together with the names of some or all of the existing partners.

o   A group name not including the names of any partners.

In each case except the first, the names of all the partners must be listed on the firm's letterheading and clearly separate from any associates, salaried partners or consultants. Since the Companies Act 1981, it is no longer necessary to register the firm name and the names of all the partners with the Registrar of Business Names.

If the group name does not contain the names of any partners, it must be recognisably architectural in character. If it is wished to use the word 'architect' in the firm name, approval must be obtained from ARCUK. The description 'chartered architects' may only be used if most partners are corporate members of the RIBA and are on the register of architects maintained by ARCUK.

8.4.7 Goodwill

Goodwill is very difficult to define. It can be said to be the benefit which a practice acquires by virtue of its prestige and the fact that clients return for further commissions. Because a partnership may be a very fluid thing, old partners leaving and new partners joining over a period of years, the prestige of the partnership may vary accordingly. If an elderly partner retires, his clients, built up over many years, may also leave and the result on the fortunes of the firm may be disastrous.

It used to be the custom for a new partner to have to buy a share in the partnership by bringing in a large capital sum. The process was usually termed 'buying a share of the goodwill'. Fig 8.1 shows, in simplified form, one way in which it could be achieved.

If the new partner could not afford to put up the initial capital sum, it was sometimes agreed that he would pay off the amount by a certain fixed agreed sum per year. That arrangement was reasonably satisfactory, provided the firm's profits steadily increased or at least remained stable during the period of paying off what was, in effect, an interest-free loan from the firm and provided that the amount per year was not too great and yet not so small that the new partner was paying back well into middle age. If he had taken out a bank loan to enable him to buy his share, his position could become untenable if profits fell. Many partners lived in near poverty for years, only achieving a good income late in life.

The situation has changed over the years so that goodwill is normally given a nil value. It has been realised that the chances of attracting a suitable young man or woman into partnership with the necessary qualifications and skills plus a large capital sum are slim. Therefore, it is usual for a suitable person to be accepted into partnership without any cash changing hands. In this situation you can expect to receive a reasonable share of the practice to ensure a good income at the time you most need it.

In return, you will be expected to leave a proportion of your earnings in the practice to build up the value of your capital account. The partners' capital accounts can be thought of as the practice's working capital. You will be entitled to draw out the full amount of your capital account, subject to any provisions in the agreement, when you leave.

There has been some resistance to this form of admitting new partners, chiefly from older partners who had to buy their shares with capital sums and who are deprived the opportunity of selling part of their shares to new partners. The problem is difficult, but in a changing economic climate it

---

Fig 8.1
Buying a share of the goodwill

Profits:	Year 1	£40,000
	Year 2	£80,000
	Year 3	£90,000
Total		£210,000

Average: $\dfrac{210,000}{3} = £70,000$

Value of goodwill: £70,000 × 2* = £140,000

Existing partners' share: X @ 60% = £84,000
Y @ 40% = £56,000

New partner buys, say, 20% share
at cost of $\dfrac{20 \times 140,000}{100} = £28,000$

X and Y might sell 10% each, thus receiving £14,000 each.
If the following year's profits were £100,000, the partners would share as follows:

X @ 50% = £50,000
Y @ 30% = £30,000
Z @ 20% = £20,000 (new partner)

* The multiplying factor is somewhat arbitrary, but it is not less than 1 and seldom more than 2.

---

must be faced squarely. Careful drafting of the partnership agreement with the advice of experienced lawyers and accountants is the answer.

8.4.8 The partnership agreement

It is usual and highly desirable that the respective rights and duties of partners be clearly set out in a formal deed of partnership properly drawn up by a solicitor and witnessed. The deed may be as long or short as is thought necessary and the partners agree. Every matter that can be anticipated should be included. If, subsequently, any circumstance arises which is not covered by the deed, the provisions of the Partnership Act 1890 and ordinary common law will apply. The result may not be what the partners intended.

If you are the incoming partner, you may be tempted to agree to use of the practice's existing professional advisers (solicitors and accountants) to prepare the agreement. The existing partners may put some pressure on you. Arguments for using one set of professional advisers are:

o   Cheaper.

o   Quicker.

o   Being professional people, they will be impartial in their advice.

Do not be tempted. It may be quicker, it may be cheaper, but since the arrangements may have to last the best part of a working lifetime, these are relatively small considerations. In most cases, the professional advisers will indeed be impartial, but impartial advisers are not really appropriate in such circumstances. It is in the best interests of all parties that separate professional advisers are used to look after respective interests.

The usual system is that the existing and incoming prospective partners have a number of informal discussions to clear the air and establish points to be agreed. Both sides should then have separate meetings with their professional advisers. After that, one or two formal meetings with all parties present should be enough to settle outstanding matters.

It sometimes happens that agreement is complete except for one item which causes difficulty. If you are the incoming partner, you must discuss the contentious matter throughly with your solicitor and, if appropriate, your accountant, in private. Take their advice. It cannot be stressed too much that you should not be tempted to agree to anything against the strong advice of your professional advisers, simply to achieve a partnership. If the point is important, standing firm will only do you good. Remember, there are other practices and other partnerships. If you have ability, you are in a strong position.

If you are an existing partner faced with the same situation, the position is slightly different. Take advice, but come to your own decision in the light

Fig 8.2

List of heads of terms which should or could be included in a
partnership agreement

Head of Term	Comment
1. Names and residence of the parties.	
2. The firm name.	See section 8.4.6.
3. Place or places of business.	
4. Date on which the partnership is to begin.	Tax considerations will have an important bearing.
5. Value of goodwill.	Usually nil.
6. The amount of capital or other assets each partner is bringing into the practice or, in the case of existing partners, how distribution of existing capital assets are to be settled including any consideration between parties.	It is common to take an inventory of all partnership assets and annex it to the deed.
7. Work in progress and how it is to be treated.	This has an important bearing on the tax position and advice should be obtained from an accountant.
8. Duties and responsibilities of partners, amount of time to be devoted to the practice, length of holidays, involvement in activities outside the partnership, dismissal and engagement of staff.	May vary between partners depending upon length of service and other considerations.

Fig 8.2 – *contd.*

Head of Term	Comment
9. Proportions in which profits or losses are to be shared between partners.	This is normally the same as the shareholding.
10. The position regarding interest on capital.	Usually no interest is given.
11. The amount of cash drawings per partner per month.	Special provisions or gurantees may be considered desirable for new partners in certain circumstances.
12. Banking arrangements including provision for signing cheques, number of signatures required, restriction on amounts.	It is often stipulated that one signature will suffice up to a certain amount, above that two or more signatures are required.
13. Retirement of partners provisions regarding money, withdrawal of capital, age.	Withdrawal provisions on retirement might include provisions for withdrawing in instalments.
14. Termination of partnerships, provisions for and length of notice, division of assets.	Assets include such things as uncompleted work, drawings, etc.
15. Rights and duties in respect of death, illness, bankruptcy.	Includes provisions for repaying capital to widow, possibly in instalments.
16. Partner being removed from register of ARCUK. Provisions to cover the position of all partners.	Includes provisions for costs, eg, changing letter heads
17. Arbitration of disputes, provisions for appointing arbitrator.	

Fig 8.2 – *contd.*	
Head of Term	**Comment**
18. Capital repayments.	
19. Partner insurance.	Usual for all partners to agree to insure one another for agreed sum payable on death to cover capital repayment to widow.
20. Professional indemnity insurance, provisions for insured amount, updating, premium payments.	
21. Partnership cars, telephone and other perks.	
22. Good faith, provisions to formally cover relations between partners and their general duty to the practice and one another.	

of your own knowledge of the existing partnership and its future prospects.

Fig 8.2 is a list of heads of terms which should or could be included in a partnership agreement. You may wish to include others to suit particular circumstances.

8.5   Directorship

If the practice is run as a limited company, you may be invited to become a director. This is equivalent to being a partner, but there are a number of important differences which have legal implications. Limited companies are dealt with in section 9.7.3. It should be noted that it is easier to remove a director than to remove a partner.

8.6　Summary

o　To decide whether you should stay in one office or move to another, ask yourself: Are you happy? If not, why not? Can you correct the situation? If so, do it; if not, move.

o　Look for increase in responsibility and salary, not just a fancy title.

o　You should expect some promotion within three years of taking up your post.

o　Be single-minded in the pursuit of objectives.

o　An associate is not the same as a partner and should never be represented as such.

o　It is dangerous to be a salaried partner.

o　An essential element of partnership is the sharing of profit or loss.

o　The greatest disadvantage of partnership is joint and several liability.

o　The provisions of the partnership agreement have no effect on third parties.

o　Consider becoming a 'man of straw'.

o　Your partnership share is ultimately determined by your value to the firm.

o　Put something by for a rainy day.

o　A failing business is the true test of a partnership.

o　Goodwill should be given a nil value.

o　There should be a formal deed of partnership.

o　Use your own solicitor and accountant.

o　Never be tempted to surrender on an important point of principle, just to enter into a partnership.

Setting up in practice

Although this book is aimed at architects in employment, it is recognised that many architects aspire to having their own practice one day. It is often achieved by working one's way up through a firm and eventually becoming a partner. The ways in which this might be accomplished have been examined in Chapter 8. Some architects, however, wish to make the leap from employment to self-employment by setting up their own business. Although the subject is outside the scope of this book, this chapter briefly summarises ways, means and motives.

There are a number of possible reasons why you may wish to start your own practice; among them:

O   You are an independent type of person who likes to be in charge of your own destiny as far as possible.

O   You think it offers you the best chance of making money.

O   You wish to produce the sort of architecture you like.

O   Your present job is unsatisfactory and you think your own practice may be the answer.

O   You just think it is the natural thing to do.

Having your own practice is rewarding, but it is hard work and you must have a strong motive in order to keep going. Therefore, starting your own practice because you think it is the natural thing to do is no reason at all. If, indeed, it is the only reason you have, stop and think carefully before you proceed further. Many people drift from one stage of their career to the next. Try not to be one of them.

Any, or any combination, of the other reasons is perfectly satisfactory. You may think that making money is an unworthy motive. But if you do not start a practice with the intention of producing a profit, you are wasting your time and you are doomed to failure.

In order to be successful – in practical terms that means making enough money to enable the practice to keep going – you must have certain attributes:

o   Health.
o   Initiative.
o   Decisiveness.
o   The ability to get on with all kinds of people.
o   Financial awareness.
o   Ability.

Those are basic requirements. Not everyone has them in equal amounts. One of the benefits of a partnership is that each partner puts in his own special talents.

It is also useful, but by no means essential, if you are a good architect. The ability to know your own strengths and weaknesses, however, is invaluable. The possession of the attributes listed above will make the difference between success and failure. If you do not have them, forget starting your own practice until either you acquire them or you meet someone who has them and who is willing to start up in business with you.

9.2   How?

9.2.1   Start the practice yourself

The most difficult, but potentially, the most rewarding both personally and financially. There is nothing quite like the feeling of creation, be it a building, a painting, a garden or an architectural practice.

The difficulties are enormous. No one actually starts from nothing. The days when one could rent an office, put up a nameplate and sit back confidently expecting clients have long gone if, in fact, they ever really existed. Before you can set up in practice on your own, you must collect two things:

o   Clients.
o   Capital.

Most sole practitioners begin by doing small jobs in their spare time. This is probably the most awkward period because site visits during normal working hours are virtually impossible if you are to be fair to your present employer. You will have to work long hours in order to build up a sizeable spare time practice. Free evenings, weekends and even holidays will become a thing of the past. You are likely to become permanently tired. For this reason alone, employers tend to frown upon spare time work. They may also suspect you of trying to build up a number of clients within the firm itself whom you will take away when you eventually break free to practice on your own.

Note that Note (c) to Rule 2.9 of the RIBA *Code of Professional Conduct* requires that:

'A member permits the architects he employs to engage in sparetime practice and to enter architectural competitions and the the employee does not do so without the knowledge of his employer, and that he acts in accordance with Rule 2.8;' (Rule 2.8 deals with your duties if you find that you have conflicting interests).

The important thing, therefore, is to inform your employer if you intend to carry on spare time practice. Do not get into a position where your personal and professional interests conflict. For example, you should not carry out work on a private basis for any clients who are also clients of your employer; you must not make use of confidential information about a client, gained through your employment, for the purposes of your private clients.

It is often said that you should accept any commission during this period because a kitchen extension for an elderly couple may lead to an office block for their entrepreneurial son. It is much more likely to lead to more kitchen extensions.

If you cannot break out of the small extension, garage and loft conversion routine, you should think twice before taking the plunge and going it alone. You would need to have a large number of such small commissions on your books to make a living.

It is much more important to build up a number of contacts, the more the better, who are likely to give you a large commission in the future. You must be prepared, when the moment arrives and you are lucky enough to secure a sizeable commission, to make the break and set up on your own. At that time, you must carefully assess your position. As a rough guide, you should have enough work to keep you busy for three months with some likely prospects thereafter.

Another way in which you can set up in practice very quickly is to win a major architectural competition. The chances of your doing that are fairly remote, but it is conceivable. Even if you do win a competition, until fees start coming in on a regular basis, you must have a clear idea as to where your living expenses are to come from.

9.2.2 Work your way up through a practice

This is not strictly setting up in practice and, unless all your partners drop dead shortly after you become a partner, it is much easier than setting up on your own. This method has been discussed in section 8.2.

9.2.3 Join an existing practice as a partner

A time-honoured way of achieving your ambition without the teething troubles of being a sole practitioner. It used to necessitate contributing a considerable sum of money to buy a share in the goodwill (see section 8.4.7).

You need to have acquired a fair degree of experience before you contemplate such a move because you will be plunged immediately into a completely different sphere of activity from that to which you are accustomed, taking a share of the ultimate responsibility for all the work and for the survival of the office.

9.3   When?

The right time to set up in practice depends on the following:
o   Availability of capital.
o   Availability of premises.
o   The accumulation of correct experience.
o   The economic climate.
o   The availability of good advice.

9.4   Where? – accommodation

9.4.1 Working from home

You will probably start by working from home, if for no other reason than that it will be cheap. Clients will not visit you, you will visit them. Your spouse will do the typing or you will have someone to come in on a two mornings a week basis.

There may, however, be tax implications if you sell your house in the future and care should be taken over the planning position. Moreover, working from home proves too distracting for some people.

9.4.2 Opening an office

Eventually, you will have to consider moving into proper office accommodation. Among points to be taken into account are the following:
o   Location.
o   Character.
o   Size.
o   Purpose.
o   Form of acquisition.

9.5   Basic equipment

A basic equipment checklist is shown in Fig 9.1. Numbers of items are not given because they will vary according to the numbers of staff and volume of work. Two basic decisions you will have to make are:

o   What is necessary?

o   How to acquire it?

Sound advice is, get the bare minimum. How you get it depends upon many factors, but the choice is really between buying and leasing, although you should not discount the possibility of making some items yourself.

Fig 9.1
Basic equipment checklist

---

o   Drawing-board and table/draughting machine

o   T-square, adjustable set square, scales, drawing pens, pencils, erasers, etc.

o   Reference table

o   Stool or drawing chair

o   Drawing storage – vertical hanging or chest or drawers

o   Desk

o   Typist's chair

o   Filing cabinet and folders

o   Typewriter – manual, electric, electronic (capable of future link to word processor for use as printer)

o   Pocket calculator

o   Portable dictating machine (with capability for use with audio typing equipment)

o   Shelving (for technical and library information)

o   Shelving (for samples)

o   Drawing print machine (if no agency near)

o   Document copying machine

o   Good quality camera

o   Dumpy level and staff

o   Ranging rods

o   Measuring tapes (steel or fabric)

o   Measuring rod

o   Manhole keys

o   Folding metal ladder

9.6 Financial management

Cash flows two ways, in and out, as follows:
o   In – mainly in the form of fees.
o   Out – capital expenditure, rents, rates, taxes, overheads, sundry purchases and salaries.
Cash flowing in must always exceed cash flowing out at any one time. It is usually assessed on a month by month basis. You must:
o   Know how much money you need.
o   Know how to get it.
o   Know what to do with it when you get it.
This involves:
o   Accurate forecasting of fee income.
o   Budgetting.
o   Control of creditors and debtors.
o   Control of work load.

9.7 Types of practice

9.7.1 Sole principal

If you opt to practise as a sole principal, there are four major results:
o   You alone will receive all profits.
o   You alone will bear all lossess.
o   You alone are liable for all mistakes.
o   You have no one with whom you can discuss problems on an equal basis.
There are other effects, of course, such as the fact that you have the final decision on all office policy. It is, however, a power which is usually sweeter in the anticipation than in the wielding. The most common observation made by sole principals is that it is a lonely life. It follows that you must be a special kind of person to make a success of, and enjoy, this method of working. Above all, you must be sufficiently self-confident to know when to stick to a decision even though circumstances may seem to be against you.
Most of the important aspects of the sole principal have already been dealt with in section 9.2.1.

9.7.2 Partnership

This type of practice has been covered in section 8.4.

9.7.3 Limited liability

A limited company is commonly taken to be a company in which liability is limited to the nominal value of the shareholding. In practice, it means that if you form a limited company and it is engulfed by some overwhelming debt, the only funds available to meet that debt will be the liquidated assets of the company, any applicable insurance cover and the amount you have put into the company as capital. If the debt remains unsatisfied, the company can be wound up and you would usually have no further liability.

The principle is best illustrated by an example: If you and your architect colleagues (say three of you) put up five hundred pounds each in order to start a company and subsequently the company is unable to meet its debts, you will have lost your five hundred pounds together with anything the company has acquired (e.g., drawing-boards, typewriters, company cars, etc.), but your personal assets will remain untouched. You and your colleagues can start a new company the following day, if you so wish, free from debt. (This situation, however, is subject to the provisions of the Insolvency Act 1985, which gives a court power to make a declaration that a director must personally contribute to a company's debts in certain circumstances. The Act, among other things, empowers a court to order disqualification of a director considered to be unfit. After insolvency liquidation, a former director may not be involved, for a period of five years, in the formation of a company with a similar name).

In forming a company, it is probable that you and your colleagues will each contribute some capital (known as your shareholding) and you will each become directors, not partners. The legal position is that you have created a separate entity, the company, and the company now employs you. You are each paid a salary by the company and if there are profits and a dividend is declared at the financial year's end, you will each receive dividends strictly in accordance with your shareholding. It is perfectly possible for some shares to be held by persons not employed by the company – your spouse for example. It is also possible to appoint to a directorship a trusted member of staff with no shares in the company. That person would receive a salary, but no year's end dividend.

The advantages of a limited company are:

○   You have no personal liability for the company's debts.

○   There is a board of directors to discuss problems and decide policy.

○   Two or more people should generate more ideas and attract more work than one (as in a partnership).

o   The company continues in being even if shares change hands (it is difficult to split up a partnership).

o   It is relatively easy to appoint or remove a director.

o   It is easier to attract additional capital to a company than to a partnership.

The disadvantages of a limited company are:

o   A company can only be formed and act in accordance with the provisions of the Companies Acts. It comes into existence only when it has been registered with the Registrar of Companies. Transactions carried out before registration could be considered, legally, as the transactions of a partnership with unlimited liability.

o   The powers of a company are limited by the 'objects clause' of its Memorandum of Association.

o   The accounts of a company must be filed with the Registrar of Companies where they may be inspected by the public.

o   There are certain statutory constraints on the running of a company, e.g., you must have at least one Annual General Meeting of all shareholders each year.

o   A company normally comes to an end by being liquidated in accordance with the Companies Acts. This is a formal and possibly lengthy process.

o   A shareholder has no power to bind the company by any of his actions unless so agreed by the board of directors and within the powers of the company as indicated in the 'objects clause'. But a shareholder has power over a company because the shareholders all together are the owners of the company. They must act within the Companies Acts and the company's 'objects clause', but, in rare situations, if they dislike the way the company is being run, they can vote to dismiss a director or go to court if, as a minority, their rights and views within the company are being overridden or ignored.

o   There is no room for discretion or agreement on the apportionment of dividends. They must be divided strictly in accordance with the shareholding.

o   As an architect director, you will pay tax on the PAYE system. There is no opportunity to take advantage of the 'self-employed' tax concessions. The general taxation position may also be worse than might exist in self-employment.

The one big advantage is, of course, limitation of liability. Disadvantages are mainly procedural. It is still perfectly possible for a client to sue any director in tort for negligence, but the consequences may not be as bad as when a partner is sued, because directors are not jointly and severally liable.

Companies can be tailor-made for your purposes by a solicitor. It is not expensive. It is even cheaper to buy a company 'off the shelf'. Shelf companies are ready-formed, the paper work is done and you can get one in a day if necessary. It can be tricky to change a partnership into a limited company and even more complicated if you change your mind and wish to revert to a partnership. The moral is to think carefully before you take the plunge.

Company law and procedure is quite complex. Your solicitor and accountant will advise. Fig 9.2 is a list of some important points concerning private limited companies.

9.7.4 Unlimited liability

An unlimited company may have a maximum of 50 members. Although they do not have any personal liability for the company's debts, they are liable to contribute in the proportion of their shareholding if the company's assets are insufficient.

The principal advantages of an unlimited company are:

o   A director becomes free of liability twelve months after leaving the company and selling his shares. He may still be sued in tort for negligence, of course, if negligence can be proved. But, in this respect, he is in the same position as the director of a limited company.

o   There is no requirement for the filing of reports and accounts, etc., with the registrar of companies. The financial affairs of the company, therefore, are shielded from the public gaze.

There is a considerable degree of formality associated with an unlimited company, however, and unless your accountant puts forward pressing reasons, there would appear to be little reason for starting a practice in this way. Unlimited companies are rare.

9.7.5 Public company and share sale

The essential difference between a private company and a public limited company is that members of the public can buy and sell the shares of the latter. There seems to be nothing wrong in principle for an architectural practice to carry on its business in this way provided that the control of the company remains in the hands of an architect. Where shares are available to the public, the possibility of control of the practice passing out of the hands of architects is considerably increased. At the time of writing, the situation is fluid, but it can be stated with a fair degree of certainty that architectural control of a practice is likely to be a key factor in any case where ARCUK is called upon to decide whether the practice is entitled to use the term 'architect' or one of its derivatives in relation to its business. Any sort of agreement to restrict the number of shares on sale to the public

Fig 9.2
Private limited companies – important points

o   Need only have one director (public companies must have at least two).

o   An undischarged bankrupt cannot be a director.

o   There must be a secretary who cannot be the same person as a sole director.

o   The secretary shares responsibility with directors for compliance with the Companies Acts and must sign the Annual Return.

o   Cannot offer shares to the public.

o   Can trade immediately after incorporation without any mimimum capital requirement.

o   There is now no limit on number of members, but if number falls below two for six months, personal liability can be incurred.

o   Must have a Memorandum including the following clauses:
Name.
Office (where registered e.g., England and Wales or Scotland).
Objects.
Liability (whether limited).
Capital.

o   Memorandum must be subscribed by at least two people taking at least one share each.

o   Name must include 'Ltd' as the last word.

o   Name cannot be registered if the same as another already on index of names, if offensive or if its use would be a criminal offence.

o   Name must appear in full on business correspondence, etc.

o   Business correspondence must also include:
List of directors or where they can be found.
Registered number and where registered.

o   Must have articles, which must be printed.

o   Articles must be signed by subscribers.

o   Other forms must be prepared to include details of directors, secretary, registered office, capital duty and statutory declaration of compliance.

Fig 9.2 – *contd.*
o   Registrar's fee must be paid on incorporation.
o   Registrar issues certificate of incorporation.
o   Must keep certain books (e.g., accounts, register of shareholders) and have a common seal.
o   Can use name other than company name provided that company name also appears on correspondence, etc.
o   A register of directors must be kept and registrar must be notified of changes.
o   A register must be kept showing interests of directors, spouses and children in the company's shares.
o   Must have a qualified independent auditor.
o   Auditor's main duty is to report to members on the accounts.
o   Must be at least one AGM every calendar year.
o   Unless otherwise agreed by all those who are entitled to attend, twenty-one clear days' notice of AGM is required.

(e.g., keeping 51% for architect directors) would be frowned on by the Council of the Stock Exchange.

Since a private limited company is not allowed to sell shares on the open market, trading as a public limited company is a useful way of raising finance. Members of the public who buy the shares receive an appropriate proportion of the profits each year and, unlike the traditional practice, their only input is the original finance and, of course, the risk. If the directors are all architects, they may well find themselves working for outside investors as well as for themselves. Public limited companies must put the status or the letters 'PLC' after the company name, and the regulations with regard to such companies are rather more stringent than for a private company. Whether all this is worth it will depend mainly on how keen you are to raise money. The procedure for selling shares in this way is a specialist operation and it is unlikely that you will contemplate this sort of arrangement as a first step – if for no other reason than that prospective buyers of your shares will require some indication of your track record and prospects before parting with cash.

9.7.6 Co-operative

In order to be registered under the Industrial and Provident Societies Acts a co-operative must consist of a minimum of seven members.
Less than seven members would have to practise as a partnership or be

incorporated as a limited or unlimited liability company under the Companies Acts.

Liability, in the case of liquidation, is limited to the value of the shareholding. Individual members usually hold shares of only nominal value. The co-operative is controlled by its members on a one person, one vote basis although, generally, a committee of management is set up. How far you consider that everyone in the firm should share responsibility and rewards will determine whether you opt for this type of practice.

9.7.7 Group practice

This is not strictly something which you would consider as an initial way of setting up in practice except in very rare instances. It is essentially a method of association with other practices for mutual benefit. Some of the advantages may be:

o   The opportunity to share accommodation and other resources.

o   The opportunity to share financial arrangements.

o   The opportunity to share expertise and knowledge.

o   Staff manoeuvrability.

There are many different ways in which a group practice can be arranged depending on the requirements of the individual firms. The essential thing is to have the arrangement formalised. This can be as complex as, and in many ways is similar to, a normal partnership agreement. There are five types of group practice:

o   The group association – two or more firms loosely linked for the purpose of sharing experience and knowledge. In this type of practice each firm has a clearly separate identity for the purpose of carrying out work, etc.

o   Shared facilities – two or more firms share accommodation, etc., and may practise together as one large firm or singly.

o   Single project group partnership – an association formed, usually, for a specific purpose. When the purpose has been accomplished (for example, the carrying out of a project which would be beyond the capabilities of any one of the group) it automatically comes to an end.

o   Group co-ordinating firm – an association for the carrying out of a large project. One firm acts as co-ordinator for the project and the other firms are responsible for invidivual portions of the scheme. The important aspect of this type of group practice is that the co-ordinating firm takes overall responsibility for the project as far as the client is concerned.

o   Group partnership – a partnership of individual firms which continue to practise separately, but combine on certain large or complex projects.

Before deciding to enter into a group arrangement, it is essential to obtain legal advice. The distribution of liabilities can be very complex.

9.7.8 Limited partnership

In this form of partnership, at least one partner must be responsible for all the liabilities of the partnership. In an architectural practice, this partner must be an architect. There can be one or more additional partners who contribute capital to the partnership and whose liability is limited to the amount of the capital they contribute provided that they have no part in the management of the partnership. Such partnerships must be registered under the Limited Partnership Act 1907.

This is a comparatively little used form of partnership whose chief advantage appears to be the possibility of using funds injected by the limited partner for which he receives an appropriate share in the profits.

9.7.9 Simultaneous activities

Note that you are allowed, subject to the provisions of *Conduct and Discipline* and, if you are a member of the RIBA, the *Code of Professional Conduct*, to practise as a combination of architect and contractor or developer or estate agent, etc. You may opt to start in practice in this way. There is little doubt that the most appropriate choice of practice in these circumstances is the limited company. You must, however, watch the requirements of the codes of conduct if your professional integrity, actual and perceived, is to be preserved.

9.8   Summary

o   If you intend to carry on spare-time practice, tell your employer.
o   When you start in practice full-time, have enough work to keep you busy for three months.
o   Carefully work out the capital you need to set up in practice.
o   Working from home may have tax and planning implications.
o   Buy or lease the minimum of equipment until you have been established for 6 months.
o   You must be a special kind of person to enjoy acting as a sole principal.
o   The big advantage of a limited company is the limitation of your liabilities.
o   An unlimited company gives some protection to you after you leave.
o   If you decide to form your practice into a public limited company, it must be always under the control of an architect and approved by ARCUK.
o   A co-operative implies total sharing of liability and decisions.

o   Group practice is a useful way of pooling resources after you are established in your own right.

o   A limited partnership may be useful if a retired architect wishes to maintain a financial interest in your firm.

o   The utmost care must be taken to uphold the professional code when carrying out simultaneous activities.

Employment law

10.1   Introduction

The law relating to employment is imperfectly understood by most people. The reason for this is probably because the common law rules have been modified to such a large extent by statute. The principal statutes are:

o   The Trade Union and Labour Relations Act 1974
o   The Employment Protection Act 1975
o   The Employment Protection (Consolidation) Act 1978
o   The Employment Act 1980
o   The Employment Act 1982

The notes in this chapter are intended for general guidance. If you encounter some problem with regard to your employment, it is wise to seek advice, from your trade union, if you have one, or from a solicitor experienced in employment law.

The very first thing to be settled is whether or not you are an employee. An employee is one who enters into a *contract of service*. Most employed architects are in this category. It is possible, however, to enter into a *contract for services*. This is the case when an architect enters into a contract with his client. The distinction is important:

o   Employment law only applies to employees.
o   Common law implied duties only apply if there is an employment situation.
o   Statutory rights apply only to employees.

In some cases, deciding whether an architect is an employee or simply an independent contractor is not easy. The courts have devised a number of tests:

o   *Control* – Has the employer control over the architect's method of carrying out the work? If so, the architect is an employee. The greater the control, the greater the likelihood that the situation is one of employment.

o   *Integration* – Does the architect form an integral part of the business? This is a useful test for the professional person where the degree of control may be limited.

o   *Multiple test*

Does the architect work for an agreed salary?

Is the degree of control sufficient so that the employer can be considered the master (i.e., is there a master and servant situation)?

Are the other contract provisions consistent with employment? (e.g., Who pays the tax? Who pays pensions? Who owns the drawing-boards, etc.?).

A contract of employment (i.e., *of service*) can be written or oral. It can also arise by conduct of the parties. Certain terms will be implied by common law unless replaced by an express term of the contract. In addition, implied terms may be implied by the conduct of the parties. The courts will not imply a term unless it is necessary to render the contract effective. It is not part of the court's duty to improve a contract.

10.2   Common law duties

10.2.1 Employer's duties

In the absence of an express term to the contrary, the general law will imply the following terms:

o   Duty to pay the employee.

o   Duty to provide work for the employee if without such work, the employee would be unable to earn any money. Failure to provide the work is a breach of contract.

o   Duty to indemnify the employee if he incurs expense reasonably in carrying out his duties.

o   Duty to take care for the employee's safety. This duty is now covered by the Health and Safety at Work Act 1974.

Suspension on full pay is not, therefore, a breach of contract, but suspension without pay normally is a breach depending on the terms of the contract.

10.2.2 Employee's duties

In the absence of an express term to the contrary, the general law will imply the following terms:

o   His service must be personal. The employee cannot delegate his duties to someone else. Clearly if you are an architect in charge of a team, you can delegate certain aspects of the work to individuals, but in doing this you are simply performing your duties. You would be in breach of contract if you delegated your own duties to another.

o   The employee must obey the lawful instructions of his employer.

o   The employee must take reasonable care when about his employer's business. If you take the opportunity, when visiting site, to attend to some business of your own and, in doing so, you cause some damage, your employer would be vicariously liable for your actions, but he would be able to recover the cost of such damage from you.

o   The employee must demonstrate good faith. He must reveal anything which is necessary to be revealed to safeguard his employer's interests and he must take care of confidential information.

10.3   Statutory duties

10.3.1 Industrial tribunals

Originary contractual rights arising at common law from a contract of employment are dealt with by the courts in the usual way. Statutory rights are enforced by industrial tribunals composed of a chairman, who is a lawyer, a member chosen from a panel nominated by the CBI and a member chosen from a panel nominated by the TUC. The tribunal has the power to decide cases and award various remedies including compensation. Appeal from an industrial tribunal lies with the employment appeal tribunal. Appeals from the employment appeal tribunal may be made, on a point of law only, to the Court of Appeal and the House of Lords. The procedure at an industrial tribunal is intended to be informal so that each party can appear without legal representation. Normally each party bears its own costs.

The application to the tribunal must be made within three months of the dismissal date, but the tribunal does have power to extend this period in certain cases.

Normally there is just one hearing, but there is provision for other applications to be made before the hearing:

o   Further and better particulars of the claim. The tribunal will rarely consent, preferring matters to remain informal.

o   Discovery. This is similar to the court's power to order all relevant documents to be revealed to the other party.

o   Order for attendance of witnesses. If granted, the witness is entitled to payment.

o   Preliminary hearing. In order to settle points which may lead to the whole application being settled without a full hearing.

○ Pre-hearing assessment. Either party may request it or the tribunal itself may decide to proceed in this way. The principle is that the tribunal hears the evidence and gives an informal opinion which, although not binding, indicates how the case may be decided at a full hearing. It is open for the parties to proceed to a full hearing, but if the decision is the same, the tribunal has power to award costs against one of the parties. Pre-hearing assessments are little used.

10.3.2 Written statement

The employee is entitled to a written statement of the principal contract terms not later than thirteen weeks after he commences employment. There are several points to note:

○ The statement must be given to the employee. It is not enough if the employer simply refers to standard conditions or pins the conditions on a notice board.

○ The statement is not the contract. The contract will have been entered into at latest when the employee took up his employment. It is, therefore, open to the employee to contend that the statement represents new terms and not those on which he was employed. It is not thought that the employee's signature on the statement (a requirement in some companies) will affect the position, not only on the principle that the employee cannot sign away his rights, but also because the signing is usually simply acknowledgement of receipt.

○ If the employer fails to supply the statement or the employee disputes any of the terms, or lack of them, either party can refer to the industrial tribunal which will make a decision incorporating the points in dispute. But that is the only sanction available. No cash is awarded. Therefore, many firms omit to supply the statement.

The statement must contain the following points:

○ Indentities of the parties.

○ Date employment commenced and if any previous period of employment counts as part of period of continuous employment for statutory protection purposes.

○ If a fixed term contract, the date on which the contract expires.

○ The job title.

○ The period of notice required to end the contract. Any period can be stipulated, but if it is less than the statutory minimum, the statutory minimum applies. If no period is stipulated, the statutory minimum does not apply and reasonable notice must be given (except under a fixed term contract).

○ Rate and intervals of pay.

o   Hours of work.

o   Holiday entitlement and holiday pay situation. There is no automatic right to holidays either in statute or under common law.

o   Pension scheme. The employee can be referred to another document.

o   If contracting out certificate is in force under Social Security Pensions Act 1975.

o   Sickness and sickness pay provisions. There is no right to sick pay under the general law, but usually some provision is made in the contract of employment. The employer is obliged to pay statutory sick pay for a period totalling twenty-eight weeks in any one year. After twenty-eight weeks, responsibility for payment of statutory sick pay lies with the Department of Health and Social Security.

o   Disciplinary rules and grievance procedures. There is no particular statutory requirement with regard to the procedures to be adopted, but ACAS has produced codes of practice which, if adopted, will tend to demonstrate to the industrial tribunal that the procedure was reasonable.

If there is no term in the contract relating to any of the above items, the fact must be stated. If there is any change, a further written statement of the particulars must be furnished by the employer within one month. The written statement need not be given at all if:

o   The original contract, containing all the terms, is in writing.

o   The employee works less than sixteen hours per week.

10.3.3 Maternity rights

A woman who is pregnant has the following statutory rights:

o   The right not to be unfairly dismissed by reason of pregnancy.

o   Six weeks' maternity pay.

o   The right to return to work after the end of the pregnancy.

o   The right to have time off work for ante-natal care.

In order to qualify for maternity pay and the right to return to work, the woman must satisfy the following criteria:

o   The reason for absence must be pregnancy.

o   She must be employed until the beginning (Sunday) of the eleventh week before the week in which the expected date of delivery falls.

o   By the beginning of the eleventh week before confinement she must have completed two years' continuous employment.

o   A minimum of twenty-one days (or as soon thereafter as reasonably practicable) before she commences her absence, she must inform the employer that she will be absent by reason of pregnancy. If she wishes to return to work, she must so state. Fulfilling this condition ensures that the woman will receive maternity pay and ensures the right to return to work.

She is not bound by her statement and she can decide not to return to work later.

o   She must produce a medical certificate if required.

The six weeks' maternity pay consists of 9/10 of normal pay less:

o   Flat rate maternity allowance received from the Department of Health and Social Security.

o   PAYE.

o   National insurance contributions.

The earnings related supplement and maternity grant from the DHSS are not deducted.

The woman is allowed to be absent for twenty-nine weeks beginning with the actual week of confinement. She has the right to return to work at any time before the end of this period provided she gives twenty-one days' notice of her intention. If the woman is too ill to return within the period, she can postpone her return for a further four weeks, but she must have indicated by written notice her intention to return before the end of the twenty-nine week period. The notice is not binding upon the employee. After forty-nine days from the beginning of the actual week of confinement, the employer may request written confirmation of intention to return to work. The employee must reply within fourteen days or she will lose her right to return. The employer can also postpone her return for four weeks after the end of the twenty-nine week period if it is not practicable to make suitable arrangements.

If it is not reasonably practicable to allow the employee to return, she may lose her rights by unreasonable refusal to accept suitable alternative employment. She has no right to return if the number of persons employed immediately before her absence was five or less, and it is not reasonably practicable to allow her to return or offer a suitable alternative.

10.3.4 Absence from work

The employee must be allowed to be absent from work under certain circumstances:

o   If he is a trades union official. Reasonable time off, with pay, is allowed to carry out duties.

o   If he is a trades union member. Reasonable time off, without pay, is allowed for all trades union activities except industrial action.

o   If he is redundant. Reasonable time off, with pay, is allowed to seek other employment.

o   If he holds public office. Reasonable time off, without pay, to carry out duties, for example, as a JP.

o   If she is pregnant. Reasonable time off, with pay, for ante-natal care.

In order to qualify the trades union must be independent of the employer and be recognised by the employer for the purpose of negotiation of pay, etc.

The following should be noted:

o   There is no statutory right to holidays with pay. The employer will be bound by whatever arrangements are made with employees, individually or as a whole.

o   Absence from work on compassionate grounds is entirely at the employer's discretion. It is good practice to include reference to it in the written statement (section 10.3.2).

o   The employee has no right to take leave without pay. Although many employees find it useful to take such leave from time to time, the employer can withhold permission.

o   The granting of additional leave entitlement linked to length of service is entirely a matter for the employer. It is common practice to do so to encourage and reward long and faithful service.

10.3.5 Discrimination

Discrimination on the grounds of age, religion, politics or membership of a trades union is not directly unlawful.

The Sex Discrimination Act 1975 lays down that an employer may not discriminate against a person because of sex or marital status. It applies to recruitment of staff, promotion and any benefits. Not only does the Act prevent direct discrimination, it also prevents any employer discriminating indirectly, for example, by laying down criteria for a post which unreasonably favours one sex. Such things as weight, height, strength and even age may fall into this category. Sex discrimination may be allowed in certain rare instances, usually on the grounds of decency or physiology if it is clear that it would be virtually impossible for a particular sex to do a certain job. Persons suffering discrimination may apply to the industrial tribunal. The tribunal may make an order to remove the discrimination or award compensation (to a maximum of £7,000 at present).

The Race Relations Act 1976 makes it unlawful to discriminate against any person, directly or indirectly, on the grounds of race, colour, nationality, ethnic or national origins. Direct discrimination consists of treating a person less favourably than another on purely racial grounds. Indirect discrimination is when the same criteria are applied to all persons, but the criteria are such that a particular racial group will have relatively greater than normal difficulty in complying. The position is complex, but rules regarding language and clothing may fall into this category depending on circumstances. Selection on racial grounds is permissible if membership of a particular racial group is a genuine occupational qualification for a post. An example would be where a person has to provide personal advice or services to a particular racial group if it would be difficult for a member of another racial group to perform the task. The Act applies to fellow employees as well as to employers.

The Equal Pay Act 1970 makes it unlawful for a woman to be treated less favourably because of her sex. It covers pay and conditions of service. If men and women do the same work under the same conditions, broadly they must be paid the same or be on the same pay scale. There may be other differences which justify differences in pay, such as age, qualification or hours of work. The Act does not entitle a woman to claim on the basis of differential. For example, if a man and a woman have different responsibilities, they may be paid differently and the woman cannot successfully claim under the Act because she considers that the difference is greater than it properly should be.

10.3.6 Employment of persons from outside the United Kingdom

The Immigration Act 1971 and the European Communities Act 1972 control the employment of persons from outside the United Kingdom. A person who is not a European Community national normally has to obtain a work permit before entering the United Kingdom to take up employment. Nationals of a member state of the European Community generally have the right to look for work, or take up a job previously obtained in the United Kingdom without a work permit. The regulations are complex and reference should be made to appropriate guidance booklets issued by the Department of Employment (see Appendix A).

10.3.7 Disabled persons

The Disabled Persons (Employment) Acts 1944 and 1958 regulate the employment of disabled persons. In general, the Acts apply only to firms with more than 19 employees. The firm must have a minimum of 3% of the total number of employee posts available for registered disabled persons. The employer's obligations are governed by the Acts and special arrangements must be made if an employer cannot meet requirements. Detailed information is available in the guidance booklet obtainable from the Department of Employment (see Appendix A).

10.4 Termination of employment – introduction

The circumstances in which the employee's employment is terminated may give rise to a number of situations:

o   Redundancy.

o   Wrongful dismissal – a breach of contract, if, for example, insufficient notice is given,

o   Unfair dismissal – a statutory concept, when proper notice is given, but the reason for dismissal is considered to be unfair.

o   Fair dismissal – when proper notice is given and the reason for dismissal is fair.

Other than fair dismissal, all the other situations may exist together. Statutory and common law provisions must be considered separately.

10.5   Termination at common law

A claim will only arise if the dismissal is wrongful. Therefore, in the following instances, no claim is possible:

o   If the contract comes to an end by genuine agreement between the two parties. The legal position is that a new contract has been entered into, by which each party is released from its obligations. From the employer's point of view, it is wisest to make the agreement under seal.

o   Operation of law. The most common situation is frustration. This can arise if the employee dies or suffers a prolonged illness, but not if the employer become bankrupt. The situation is only really relevant to fixed term contracts. In other cases, proper notice is all that is required.

o   Effluxion of time. This only applies to a contract for a fixed term. When the term expires, the employee is automatically dismissed. However, if the contract is not renewed, there may be grounds for a statutory unfair dismissal claim.

o   Notice. If the contract is for a fixed term, it cannot be ended by notice. If the contract is open-ended or for a fixed term with a break clause, it can be ended by reasonable notice unless the period of notice is specified in the contract, in which case the notice must not be less than the statutory minimum.

The statutory minimum periods of notice which must be given by the employer are:

One week, if continuously employed for more than one month, but less than two years.

Thereafter, one week for every complete year worked (maximum twelve weeks).

The employee can, of course, waive his right to notice and take wages in lieu. It is not thought that the employer can force the employee to take wages in lieu of proper notice, but a court would not be likely to award a greater sum in the event of a claim.

The only statutory obligation on the employee with regard to notice is to give one week's notice if employed for more than four weeks.

The employee can be dismissed without notice if he is in breach of his contract. In effect, the employer is saying that the employee has repudiated the contract by reason of misconduct and the employer is accepting the termination. Misconduct can take the form of stealing from the firm, fighting or total incompetence. Disobedience may be sufficient grounds, depending on the terms of the contract (i.e., job title, responsibilities). If gross misconduct is found to have taken place before the dismissal, even if the dismissal was effective before the discovery, it will probably be a good defence for the employer against a claim for wrongful dismissal.

If the dismissal is wrongful, the employer is liable for damages. It is impossible completely to separate common law and statutory factors. The damages will be assessed on the basis of an intention to place the employee in the same position he would have been in if the contract had been properly performed. Therefore, in the case of a fixed term contract, the damages may be equivalent to the total salary lost for the remainder of the term due to the dismissal. If the contract is open-ended or for a fixed term with a break clause, the damages are likely to be the amount of salary payable during whatever period of notice is applicable or, if no specific period, during a reasonable period (not to be less than the statutory minimum). The amount of damages may be increased to take account of such things as benefits usually enjoyed (car, pension, luncheon vouchers, etc.). The damages payable may be reduced in certain instances;

○ If the employee has not attempted to mitigate his loss by, for example, finding alternative employment or even taking another job with the same employer (the court, however, will take into account whether it is reasonable to go back to the same employer in the particular circumstances).

○ If a straight calculation of damages shows that the employee is receiving money in advance of the anticipated date (this might be the case with a fixed term contract). This is likely to be a rare occurrence.

○ If there are benefits which reduce the apparent loss. This category includes such things as unemployment and supplementary benefit and an unfair dismissal award. It is not clear whether a redundancy payment must be deducted, but the balance of opinion seems to indicate not. The damages will also be reduced by the amount of tax and national insurance payments which would have been paid had there been no dismissal.

The employee has six years in which to make a claim for wrongful dismissal.

10.6   Termination – statutory procedures

10.6.1 Disciplinary procedures

The precise discipinary procedures can be extremely important if the employer is to avoid a claim for unfair dismissal. The general process is as follows:

o   The procedure should be stated in writing.

o   The procedure should be quick.

o   The employer should state what action he can take.

o   The person who can operate the procedure should be specified and the degree of consultation among them established.

o   There should be a formal warning procedure consisting of one oral and one written warning followed by something less than dismissal before dismissal takes place.

o   With the exception of gross misconduct, a first offence should not incur dismissal.

o   The employee should be informed of the complaint against him and have someone to represent him. This other person may be simply a friend or a trades union official.

o   There should be some system of appeal.

10.6.2 Redundancy and unfair dismissal

The following section applies to both redundancy and unfair dismissal. Certain criteria must be satisfied:

o   Employee must be under 65. If the dismissal is alleged to be unfair, the employee must be less than the usual retiring age in that particular job.

o   Employee must not belong to a class of workers excluded by statute, e.g., registered dock worker, police, etc.

o   The employment must be continuous with one employer. An exception to this is where the business is transferred from one employer to another.

The employee must work at least sixteen hours each week or be contracted to do so.

If the work runs out through no fault of the employee it is not counted as a break in employment, no matter how long it lasts.

If there is a strike, it does not rank as a break, but the period of the strike cannot count towards the period of continuous employment.

Where short-time working of less than twenty-six weeks' duration is introduced for employees working over sixteen hours a week, the period is counted and there is no break provided that the short time is over eight hours per week.

If a probationary period is stipulated as part of the terms of employment, it will count as part of the period of continuous employment provided the appointment is confirmed. Probationary periods are neither prescribed nor prevented by statute. They are purely matters to be agreed between employers and employees. Common periods are three and six months.

o   The employee must have been dismissed. There are basically three situations;

The employer terminates the contract.

The employee terminates the contract as in constructive dismissal. This is where the employer acts in such a way as to repudiate the contract and the employee simply accepts the repudiation.

A fixed term contract comes to an end without renewal. This may still be considered dismissal.

o   The employee must not ordinarily work outside Great Britain.

10.6.3 Redundancy and payments

If the dismissal is because of redundancy, the employee is entitled to redundancy payment. In addition to the criteria in section 10.6.2, the following criteria must be satisfied;

o   The employee must be at least eighteen years old.

o   The employee must have completed two years of continuous employment on the day he leaves. If no notice is given the statutory period of notice is added on to the actual period worked to determine eligibility.

The establishment of redundancy can be a complicated business. It may be enough that the employer's requirement for an operative has ceased. A distinction is made between the post and the employee. If, for example, the job for which the employee was engaged has ceased to exist, perhaps because of a declining market, there could be a redundancy situation. If, on the other hand, the job had ceased in one area, but still exists in a different geographical area and the employee has a clause in his contract permitting the employer to transfer him, refusal to transfer on the part of the employee would not create redundancy, but probably fair dismissal.

If the employer offers to re-engage the employee, there are a number of important aspects to consider:

o   If the offer is made more than four weeks from the redundancy there is a redundancy situation, the employee is entitled to redundancy pay and he is treated as having started a new job. His period of continuous employment begins afresh.

o   If the offer is made within four weeks of the redundancy:

The employee is not entitled to redundancy payment and the period of continuous employment continues, bridging over the short period between redundancy and re-engagement.

If the employee unreasonably refuses the offer, he will probably lose his redundancy entitlement.

If the employee accepts, he has a trial period of four weeks from the actual start of the new post. If he gives notice himself within the trial period, the situation reverts to one of redundancy. If he gives notice after the trial period, he is not entitled to redundancy payment or any other claim. If the employer gives notice during the trial period, the situation becomes one of redundancy again, but if he gives notice outside the trial period, it is in the same category as if there had been no original redundancy and no re-engagement and trial period. The employee may have a claim depending upon the circumstances.

If the employee is guilty of gross misconduct either before or after the redundancy notice has been issued, he may forfeit his redundancy payment. The law is complex and the precise circumstances of each case must be considered.

There is a presumption, which it is for the employer to attempt to disprove if he wishes, that:

o   If dates of the employee starting and finishing the job are known, that it is a period of continuous employment.

o   If the employee is dismissed, that it is because of redundancy.

The employer has six months in which to make the redundancy payment to the employee and inform the Secretary of State in order to receive a rebate. The employee also has six months in which to make an application to the industrial tribunal if he is aggrieved. In cases where the employer is slow to pay, the employee can preserve his right by making a written claim to the employer within the six month period. The employee will be paid from the Redundancy Fund if the employer is in liquidation before payment.

Payment is calculated on the basis of one week's pay (maximum £140) for every complete year of employment from the age of eighteen (maximum period twenty years). The employer can, of course, pay more, but he is not entitled to rebate in respect of the additional sum.

There are also provisions requiring the employer to consult with the appropriate trades union and to notify the Secretary of State about proposed redundancies, subject to certain time limits and numbers of employees involved. Failure to observe the proper procedure may render the employer liable to penalties.

10.6.4 Unfair dismissal

If the dismissal is unfair, the employee has the right to make a claim to the industrial tribunal. In addition to the criteria set out in section 10.6.2, the employee must have completed one year of continuous employment unless the total number of employees was twenty or less for the whole of the period, in which case the period is extended to two years.

The employer can show that the dismissal was fair if there was a substantial reason such as gross misconduct, inability to carry out the work, redundancy or illegality, etc.

The statutes have introduced the concept of dismissal for an 'inadmissable reason'. If proved, the employer has no defence and the dismissal is automatically unfair. The criteria to be satisfied by the employee are reduced and age and the period of continuous employment are of no consequence. The following is a brief summary of the circumstances involving dismissal for an 'inadmissible reason'. Dismissal because of:

○   Belonging or refusing to belong to a trades union (where there is no agreement between employer and employees regarding union membership).

○   (If there is a union membership agreement) failing to join a union specified in the agreement because:

Employee objects on grounds of conscience or deeply held personal conviction.

The possibility of industrial action would conflict with the employee's professional code.

Employee was employed before the agreement.

The industrial tribunal has ruled that the employee was unreasonably expelled or excluded or the employee has lodged a complaint to that effect.

The agreement was made after 15 August 1980 and it has not been approved or it has been approved but the employee has not been a member since the date of the ballot.

Dismissal will not be unfair if it is by reason of redundancy, but the precise circumstances will be important. National security is another reason which will make a dismissal fair, provided a certificate is obtained.

Dismissal on account of pregnancy will be unfair unless the employer can show that the pregnancy caused the woman to be unable to perform her duties and there was no suitable alternative job which she would accept.

If a strike is in progress, the situation is as follows:

○   The employer can appoint a particular day and dismiss those who have not returned to work on that day while retaining those employees who return to work. Those dismissed have no claim for unfair dismissal.

○   If the employer dismisses all those on strike and re-engages some within three months, those not re-engaged have a claim for unfair dismissal provided the claim is brought within three months.

10.6.5 Remedies

The remedies for unfair dismissal are obtained by applying to the industrial tribunal. Application must generally be made within three months of the date of termination of employment. The tribunal can order:

○   Reinstatement – To put the employee in the same position as if he had not been dismissed.

○   Re-engagement – To give the employee an equivalent post to the one he has lost.

o   Compensation – In addition to the above or instead of it.
The tribunal can also make additional orders regarding matters connected with the dismissal, such as pension rights, seniority, etc. If the employer does not comply with an order to reinstate or re-engage, the tribunal can only order compensation, which may be punitive unless the employer can show good reason why he was unable to reinstate or re-engage.

10.6.6 Calculation of compensation

The awards and maximum payments are as follows:

Basic award	£4,200
Compensatory award	£7,500
Additional award	£3,640 or £7,280
Special award	no maximum

Basic award
The employer can receive 1½ weeks' pay (maximum £140 per week allowed as pay, therefore maximum in this instance is £210 per week) for each complete year over the age of forty-one; 1 week's pay for each complete year between twenty-two and forty-one and half a week's pay for each complete year under twenty-two. Maximum number of years taken into account is twenty.
The basic award may be reduced:
o   By 1/12 for every month the employee is less than a year from retiring age. For example a man who is 64 years and 2 months will have his award reduced by 2/12.
o   By the amount of redundancy payments if applicable.
o   By a discretionary amount if the employee is guilty of misconduct or has unreasonably refused the employer's offer of reinstatement.

Compensatory award
The industrial tribunal can award whatever it feels is just and equitable in all the circumstances. Maximum – £7,500.

Additional award
In appropriate cases it will be between thirteen and twenty-six weeks' pay (maximum pay taken as £140 per week). If the dismissal was by reason of sex or racial discrimination, the award may be between twenty-six and fifty-two weeks' pay. The industrial tribunal has power to decide the amount.

Special award
If this award is made, the 'additional award' is not payable. A special award is made in instances where the dismissal was for an 'inadmissible reason':

o   If reinstatement is not ordered, the employee can receive 104 weeks pay (there is no maximum pay per week), subject to a minimum of £10,000 and a maximum of £20,000.

o   If reinstatement or re-engagement is ordered and the employer does not comply, the employee can receive 156 weeks' pay (no maximum pay per week) subject to a minimum of £15,000.

10.7   Health and safety

There are a considerable number of Acts of Parliament and regulations made under them, aimed at achieving a high standard of health and safety in relation to work. The principal Act is now the Health and Safety at Work Act 1974. The Act covers all persons at work, whether they are employers, employees or self-employed with the exception of domestic servants in a private household. In addition, protection is given to members of the public who may be affected by work activities.

The storage and use of dangerous substances and all airborne emissions of obnoxious or offensive substances are controlled including substances not being used in connection with work, and airborne emissions which, while not dangerous, are a nuisance or would cause damage to the environment.

A key objective of the Act is to involve both management and workforce in achieving high standards of health and safety. The regulations are detailed. Some of the principal points are as follows;

The employer must:

o   Ensure as far as reasonably practicable, the health, safety and welfare at work of all employees.

o   Provide and maintain plant and systems of work which are, so far as is reasonably practicable, safe and without risk to health.

o   Provide such information, instruction, training and supervision as is necessary to ensure, so far as is reasonably practicable, the health and safety at work of his employees.

o   Maintain any place of work under his control in a safe condition so far as is reasonably practicable and provide and maintain safe means of access and egress.

o   Provide, so far as is reasonably practicable, a safe working environment without risks to health and adequate as regards facilities and arrangments for welfare of employees while at work.

o   Prepare and revise as often as appropriate a written statement of general policy with regard to health and safety at work for employees and the arrangements currently in force for carrying out the policy, and bring the statement and any revisions to the notice of all employees.

o   Provide arrangements for safety representatives and safety committees.

o   Conduct his undertakings so as to ensure as far as is reasonably practicable, that no person not in his employ who may be affected is exposed to risks to health or safety.

The employee must;

o   Take reasonable care for his own health and safety and the health and safety of other persons who may be affected by his acts or omissions.

o   Co-operate with the employer as necessary to enable statutory requirements or duties to be complied with.

It is prohibited to charge any employee in respect of anything done or provided in order to comply with the health and safety regulations.

Inspectors are appointed to ensure that the Act is being observed. An inspector may:

o   Enter any premises, at a reasonable time, if he has reason to believe that it is necessary for him to enter in order to carry out his duties.

o   Be accompanied by any person duly authorised.

o   Take any equipment, take measurements and photographs.

o   Take samples.

o   Require persons to give information.

o   Require any person to assist him within the scope of the person's responsibilities.

If the inspector finds a contravention of the Act, he may;

o   Issue a prohibition notice requiring the activity to stop. This notice is usually issued if there is a risk of serious personal injury.

o   Issue an improvement notice requiring the fault to be remedied within a specified time.

o   Prosecute any person contravening a relevant statutory provision. The prosecution can be summary in a magistrate's court or on indictment in the Crown court. The maximum fine for summary conviction is, at present, £400. For conviction on indictment there is no maximum fine and the possibility of imprisonment for up to two years in certain cases.

o   Seize or destroy anything he considers to be dangerous.

Appeal can be made against a notice, by the person receiving it, to an industrial tribunal.

10.8   Summary

Since the purpose of this chapter is to summarise the employment law, no useful summary can be attempted. In a dismissal situation, it is crucial that you obtain expert advice as quickly as possible. If you are a director of a company, the position is further complicated and no useful purpose can be served by attempting to condense the factors to be taken into account.

Bibliography

2 Professional duties
ARCUK *Conduct and discipline* (1981)
RIBA *Code of Professional Conduct* (1984)
Cornes, R. L. *Professional Liability in the Construction Industry.*
Collins, London, 1984

3 Obtaining employment
Dowding, H. and Boyce, S., *Getting the Job You Want.* London, 1979, Ward Lock
Kelly's Manufacturers and Merchants Directory. Kelly's Directories, East Grinstead, 1985
Key British Enterprises. Dunn and Bradstreet, London, 1983
RIBA Guide to Employment Practice. RIBA Publications Ltd, London, 1986
Sell's Directory. Sell's Publications Ltd, Epsom, 1985
UK Trade Names. Kompass Publishers Ltd, East Grinstead, 1984/5

4 Basic office skills
Chappell, D. *Report Writing for Architects.* The Architectural Press Ltd, London, 1984
Chappell, D. *Standard Letters in Architectural Practice.* The Architectural Press Ltd, London, 1987
Chappell, D. *Standard Letters for Building Contractors.* The Architectural Press Ltd, London, 1987
Cooper, B. M. *Writing Technical Reports.* Penguin, Harmondsworth, 1964
Hargrave, R. *Office Library Systems.* The Architectural Press Ltd, London, 1987

5 Specific architectural skills
Porter, T and Greenstreet, B. *Manual of Graphic Techniques.* vol 1, The Architectural Press Ltd, London, 1980

Porter, T and Goodman, S. *Manual of Graphic Techniques*. vols 2, 3, and 4, The Architectural Press Ltd, London, 1982/5
Willis, A. J. and Willis, C. J. *Specification Writing for Architects and Quantity Surveyors*. Collins, London, 1983
Woods, F. and Powell, J. *Overlay Drafting*. The Architectural Press Ltd, London, 1986

6 Work in progress
Chappell, D. *Contractor's Claims*. The Architectural Press Ltd, London, 1984
Chappell, D. *Contractual Correspondence for Architects*. The Architectural Press Ltd, London, 1983
Chappell, D. and Powell-Smith, V. *JCT Intermediate Form of Contract*. The Architectural Press Ltd, London, 1985
Chappell, D, and Powell-Smith, V. *JCT Minor Works Form of Contract*. The Architectural Press Ltd, London, 1986
Green, R. *The Architect's Guide to Running a Job*. The Architectural Press Ltd, London, 1986
Greenstreet, B. *Legal and Contractual Procedures for Architects*. The Architectural Press Ltd, London, 1984
Jones, G. P. *A New Approach to the 1980 Standard Form of Building Contract*. Longman, London, 1980
Parris, J. *The Standard Form of Building Contract JCT 1980*. Collins, London, 1985
Powell-Smith, V. and Chappell, D. *Building Contracts Compared and Tabulated*. The Architectural Press Ltd, London, 1987
Watts, J. W. *The Supervision of construction: a guide to site inspection*. Batsford, London, 1980

7 Achieving objectives
Drucker, P. F. *Managing for Results*. Pan, London, 1967
Drucker, P. F. *The Effective Executive*. Pan, London, 1968
Vroom, W. *Work and Motivation*. John Wiley, New York, 1964

8 Climbing the ladder
Drake, C. D. *Law of Partnership*. Sweet & Maxwell, London, 1983

9 Setting up in practice
Golzen, G. *How Architects Get Work*. The Architectural Press Ltd, London, 1984
Hartley, W. C. F. *An Introduction to Business Accounting for Managers*. Pergamon Press, Oxford, 1980
Moxley, R. *The Architect's Guide to Fee Negotiation*. The Architectural Press Ltd, London, 1984

Pearce, J. *Running Your Own Co-operative.* Kogan Page, London, 1984

10 Employment law
Anderman, S. *Law of Unfair Dismissal.* Butterworth, London, 1985
Drake, C. *The Trade Union Acts.* Sweet & Maxwell, London, 1985
Drake, C. and Wright, F. *Law of Health and Safety at Work, The New Approach.* Sweet & Maxwell, London, 1983.
Meehan, E. *Women's Rights at Work.* Macmillan, London, 1985
Munkman, J. *Employer's Liability at Common Law.* Butterworth, London, 1985
Selwyn, N. *Law of Employment.* Butterworth, London, 1985
Selwyn, N. *Law of Health and Safety at Work.* Butterworth, London, 1982

Useful bookets are obtainable as follows:

From Commission for Racial Equality –

Code of Practice: for the Elimination of Racial Discrimination and the Promotion of Equality of Opportunity in Employment.

From Department of Employment –

Industrial Tribunal Procedure.
A Guide for Workers from Abroad.

Regarding employment legislation –

Employers Obligations: Disabled Persons (Employment) Acts 1944 and 1958
1 Written statement of main terms and conditions.
2 Procedure for handling redundancies.
3 Employee's rights on insolvency of employer.
4 Employment rights for the expectant mother.
5 Suspension on medical grounds under health and safety regulations.
6 Facing redundancy? – time off for job hunting or to arrange training.
7 Union membership rights and the closed shop.
8 Itemized pay statement.
9 Guarantee payments.
10 Employment rights on the transfer of an undertaking.
11 Rules governing continuous employment and a week's pay.
12 Time off for public duties.
13 Unfairly dismissed?
14 Rights to notice and reasons for dismissal.
15 Union secret ballots.
16 Redundancy payments.

From Equal Opportunities Commission –

Code of Practice.

From the Health and Safety Executive –

The Act outlined.
Advice to employees.
Advice to the self-employed.
Advice to employers.
Regulations Approved Codes of Practice and Guidance Literature.
Safety Committee.
Time off for the training of Safety Representatives.
Writing a safety policy statement: Advice to employers.
Reporting a Case of Desease.
Reporting an Injury or a Dangerous Occurrence.
Securing compliance with health and safety legislation at work.
Standards significant to health and safety at work.

From the Department of Health and Social Security –

Retiring?
Your retirement pension.
Your retirement pension if you are widowed or divorced.
Retirement benefits for married women.
Non-contributory retirement pension for people over 80.
Retirement pensions and widows' benefits: Payment direct into bank or building society accounts.
Earning extra pension by cancelling your retirement.
Which benefit?

General reference books

Handbook of Architectural Practice and Management. RIBA Publications Ltd, 1980
Job Book. RIBA Publications Ltd, 1983
Cecil, R. *Professional Liability*. The Architectural Press Ltd, London, second edition 1986
Powell-Smith, V. and Chappell, D. *Building Contract Dictionary*. The Architectural Press Ltd, London, 1985
Speight, A. and Stone, G. *AJ Legal Handbook*. The Architectural Press Ltd, London, 1985
Turner, J. H. *Architectural Practice and Procedure*. Batsford, London, 1974
Willis, A. J. and George, W. N. B. *The Architect in Practice*. Collins, London, 1981

Useful addresses of professional bodies

Architects Registration Council of the United Kingdom
73 Hallam Street
London, W1N 6EE

British Institute of Architectural Technicians
397 City Road
London, EC1V 1NE

British Institute of Interior Design
1c Devonshire Avenue
Beeston
Nottingham, NG9 1BS

Chartered Institute of Arbitrators
69–75 Cannon Street
London, EC4N 5BH

Chartered Institute of Building
Englemere
King's Ride
Ascot
Berkshire, SL5 8BJ

Chartered Institution of Building Services
Delta House
222 Balham High Road
London, SW12 9BS

Faculty of Architects and Surveyors
15 St Mary Street
Chippenham
Wiltshire

Incorporated Association of Architects and Surveyors
Jubilee House
Billing Brook Road
Weston Favell
Northampton, NN3 4NW

Institution of Building Control Officers
The White House
Carshalton Road
Sutton
Surrey, SM1 4TA

Institution of Civil Engineers
Great George Street
London, SW1P 3AA

Institution of Structural Engineers
11 Upper Belgrave Street
London, SW1X 8BH

Landscape Institute
12 Carlton House Terrace
London, SW1Y 5AH

Royal Institute of British Architects
66 Portland Place
London, W1N 4AD

Royal Institution of Chartered Surveyors
12 Great George Street
Parliament Square
London, SW1P 3AD

Royal Town Planning Institute
26 Portland Place
London, W1N 4BE

Society of Industrial Artists and Designers
Nash House
12 Carlton House Terrace
London, SW1Y 5AH

Index